About this time

JUDY WHITFIELD

This is a book of personal recollections, and as memories can be distorted by time, there are bound to be some inaccuracies. I have checked everything as much as I can, but if some of the 'shadows have offended', then let us agree I could have just dreamt it all.

ISBN-13: 978-1977897145

For my dear children
Steven, Oliver and Cassie
with love

About this time

CHAPTERS & CONTENTS

	TITLE		PAGE

Prologue

Sunny Sloane Square

A breeze caught my hair as I stepped out into the autumn morning. The rumble of London's traffic changed to a roar as I turned the corner into Sloane Street.

One minute later I was crossing a sunny Sloane Square where leaves had already fallen. I had a fleeting thought of Dick Whittington and streets paved with gold.

There was the Royal Court Theatre!

I wanted to do a twirl and shout, 'I made it - I'm here!'

Instead I stood still for a second and thought the words. Then I crossed the road to the tube station to find my way to Swiss Cottage and the Central School of Speech and Drama.

If you would like to know how I realised my dream then read on...

Tuesday's Child

1941-1947

I was born in Longton, Stoke on Trent on Tuesday 16 December 1941. There was no National Health Service then and the hospital bill for my mother's fifteen day confinement was £12 and one shilling.

My father was always known as 'Hector', but his full name was Frederick Charles Hector Taylor. My mother was Winifred Maude Taylor (née Stevens, her professional name as a dancer) and friends called her 'Wyn'.

At the time of my birth my father was in the Royal Air Force Volunteer Reserve, teaching young men, who were so desperately needed, to fly. My mother was alone much of the time, but she found support in the company of good friends. These included an already experienced mother, known to all as Mrs Plunkett, a cheerful, plump, Scottish woman who became one of my godmothers. The other was a Mrs Lawton. I cannot recall her, but she remembered my birthday for many years.

My mother's mother wasn't around much in my very early days. An incendiary bomb landed on her house in Kew in September 1941 and she promptly fled from London to take up residence next door to her sister, my Great Aunt Alice, in Lancing, Sussex.

I was told there was some discussion of my name as I was originally to be Pamela Mary Taylor, but apart from modern feminine connotations, the initials PMT were also on the buses of the local Potteries Motor Traction company. So I became Judith Elisabeth Taylor, the initials of which must have greatly pleased my aviator father. Mrs Plunkett apparently remonstrated against the choice saying, 'How can you call that beautiful baby Judith? She was that terrible woman in the Bible who cut off a man's head.'

Well, I don't seem to have been too badly influenced by the decision, as all the men in my life have left in one piece.

My earliest memories are of being in my cot in a variety of bedrooms and one particular white cottage. My father was moved from airfield to airfield so we had thirteen different homes before I was four.

Some of those were extended stays with my mother's mother, Big Granny, who was a lovely, rather fat woman who lived near the sea in Lancing, Sussex. One night when my father was away, a mine exploded on the beach, which was followed by a loud bang coming from the room where I was sleeping. My mother rushed in to find that a ventilation brick had been blown in by the blast and just missed my cot.

Later, I do remember lying in bed with a bolster tucked down the side to stop me falling out as I had nightmares of aeroplanes taking off at night and flying around the room like giant humming moths.

For a while, when we stayed in Sherston, there was a village girl called Dorothy who took me out in the pram. Mummy said I screamed and cried a lot and she could hear me from far away when Dorothy walked me around the village. Dorothy's family had a big cat which slept in the oven. I was told I must have found this fascinating as the sight of it silenced me completely.

Another reference to my fractious nature is that one evening my parents went out and left me in the care of Mummy's father. When they returned, my grandfather was playing the piano and my carry cot (with me in it) was on top of the piano.

He announced to them, 'She will learn to enjoy music!' and carried on playing. I was never told if I cried more or was soothed by his performance. This was one of the very few times I ever spent with my grandfather, as he and Big Granny were divorced by then.

I did learn to enjoy music, but it still saddens me that I have no memories of him. He was undoubtedly a man of outstanding capabilities, who started off as an electrical engineer, then took to the design side of developing air-craft engines. Among his many other pursuits, he was a skilled yachtsman, a gifted painter and a fine pianist and musician. Mummy told me that if he went to a concert and heard a piece he particularly liked, he could make

4.

notes on his shirt cuff and play it when he came home.

Apparently I did not eat enough and the doctor said to my mother, 'This child is suffering from malnutrition.' So a meal of wartime rations became a time of games played with scrambled egg made from dried eggs, mashed potato and spam and drawing pictures with tinned blackcurrant purée on home made custard. I remember being told to pretend to be a giant and swallowing food called 'rabbits' that took my open mouth for their rabbit holes.

As I became more mobile I became more adventurous and on one occasion I climbed on a chair by the bathroom sink and tried to shave myself with Daddy's razor. I cut my nose and there was a lot of blood. Mummy was very upset.

While still living in Sherston, I clearly remember sitting at the top of the stairs and falling, tumbling bumpy bump to the bottom; and one night, when my father was away in Canada, Mummy was frightened by the sound of someone at the front door trying to get in.

The next morning there was a pile of spent matches on the porch mat. A neighbour suggested it might have been a drunken serviceman who had come to the wrong house and lit match after match in an effort to see where the keyhole was. Happily, the night visitor never returned.

I also remember talk about a tank that had gone through a shop window in Malmesbury as the streets were too narrow and Mummy said it was a shame.

When Daddy returned from training pilots in Canada, he brought home bars of Fry's cream chocolate in his little brown leather suitcase. He brought other goodies in the rest of his luggage as there is an entry in my *Year by Year Story of our Baby Book.*

In Daddy's handwriting, next to my third birthday, is his entry: *Tea party: jellies, crackers, iced cake etc, brought from Canada.* These were treats that were almost impossible to find in the shops at home.

Gradually, the memories my mother told me gave way to events I can recall myself. Odd fragments still come to mind: The house in Aldershot with a front gate shaped like the setting sun, where my father's parents,

Little Granny, a small, bespectacled Irishwoman and Granddad, a tall bony man with a soldier's bearing, lived. I close my eyes and I can still see him and Daddy playing some silly game to do with flicking corks off bottles.

I also remember the level crossing at Lancing station, where the man turned a big wheel to open and close the gates and pulled tall levers to change the points. If we stood on top of the footbridge over the railway lines, when the trains went underneath we disappeared in the sulphurous smoke.

In summertime, I especially remember the lovely hollyhock flowers in Big Granny's garden and the red ants that bit me on the legs and hid under the stones.

In Lancing, I was scared of walking past the sunken entrances to air raid shelters because my father had once told me that tigers lived down there. Fortunately we never needed to seek refuge and face the terrible occupants.

Once, Daddy took me to look at the sea, but we could not walk on the pebbles or paddle because everywhere there were rolls of barbed wire and massive concrete blocks to keep invading tanks from landing - and the beaches were mined.

My father was often away from home, but I have some memories of him in those days. He was quite tall and had black hair with a parting. He looked very handsome in his RAF uniform. When he dressed in his civilian clothes he wore a long raincoat and a trilby hat and he always wore a wrist-watch. He was a very skilled pilot and trainer of pilots, but at home he drew me little pictures and put on funny voices to tell stories.

I remember my mother, who had been a showgirl, as always being kind and smiling. She was pretty, had soft brown hair and liked singing nursery rhymes and other songs like *Run Rabbit, Run,* and *Pack Up Your Troubles.* Sometimes she picked me up and danced me round the room. She always looked smart and often wore lipstick.

At the end of the war there was a procession in Lancing when all the soldiers and airmen dressed up in big carnival masks and everyone was very happy. But I was terrified of one particular figure. Someone said, 'Take your mask off, you are frightening the child,' and the man obliged - at which point I screamed even more - just as I did at Mother Goose when we went to see the pantomime at the Brighton Hippodrome.

I know this was a matinee performance on the 29 December 1945 as I still have the programme. It cost 2d, and we sat in what was called a 'back box' for 26 shillings. Undeterred by my loud hysterics at the sight of Mother Goose, early the next year my parents took me to the picture shows of *Alice in Wonderland*, and *The Wizard of Oz*, by which time I must have recovered from my pantomime trauma.

We frequently went to a news theatre. News theatres were small cinemas that had short programmes about an hour long. Sometimes they showed a travel film, a cartoon or maybe a Laurel and Hardy film, but always current news. There were also many images of a world recovering from the war which I couldn't really understand.

2

The Baby Book

In the *Baby Book* there are references to birthday presents. On my first birthday Daddy gave me a truck of bricks and some books, and Mummy gave me one of the several siren suits I wore through my young childhood. A siren suit was a cosy all-in-one item with a hood, designed for the quick dressing of children in the middle of the night when the sirens sounded and refuge had to be taken in an air raid shelter.

I was also given savings stamps, clothes, soft toys and 'dollies'. At some time I was given a Teddy Bear, who growled when his tummy was pressed; he was around for ages - even until I had my own children. There are no entries at all to my second birthday, but on my third, I received books, a monkey counter and a mackintosh. Dorothy gave me a parrot and an aunt gave me a dog next to which my father had written: *stuffed*. Presumably the parrot was too.

During my infant years I acquired several '*dollies*' from Little Granny. These must have been 'Crinoline Dolls,' some of which she made. They could stand on their own as they were held up by their hooped skirts. *Tiddlywinks* and *Pencil Box* were among fourth birthday presents, but when it came to my fifth, there was such a long list of guests I think my father must have got fed up with writing all their names down and next to Gifts was simply : '*Books, Games, Dressing Gown, money etc..*'

One gift from them which I still have, although in a very battered state, was *My First Book of Prayers*. Inside, my father has written the gift message which is dated 1 June 1945.

I was told that my parents went to a lot of trouble to find me a doll's pram, but I decided to use it for books. They told me to be careful not to squash my dolls and teddy bear with my books but they laughed when I did.

In 1945 we moved into a bungalow in North Lancing on Upper Boundstone Lane. It was new, but unoccupied, as the people who owned it could not move in. They did not want squatters, so they rented it to my father.

Finally, during the early post-war years, the mines and barbed wire were removed from the beach at Lancing and I went down to the sea with Daddy. He said we could be the first people to have stood on the beach for all the war years. Eventually, the beaches were cleared and the gaps between the concrete blocks were filled in. Later, grass was grown over them and you would never know they had ever been there.

Sometime in late 1945, my father was away and we were staying with Big Granny as my mother was heavily pregnant. It was about this time I was to start at preparatory school in the January of 1946, when I was only just four years old. Mummy was still in hospital after my brother Michael was born and she was very worried about who was going to take me to school.

As my father was away, the task was assigned to Big Granny, who was inclined to be rather nervy. When we arrived at the school gate my grand-mother's anxious hovering seemed unnecessary, so I turned to her and said: 'Go home Granny.'
And she did.

Apparently, my parents had also been worried that I would be jealous of my baby brother being at home while I was at school, but their fears were unwarranted; I loved Michael from his very beginning and still do.

I was enrolled in the Kindergarten of Lancing Preparatory School next to the small Methodist church, where I remember singing the lullaby, 'We will rock you' in the Christmas concert.

Although they put a pencil in my right hand in the class room, they did not mind when I preferred to use my left. I learned my tables there and we said, 'twice times' instead of 'two times' which made me come a cropper at my next school.

We must have stayed for quite a while with Big Granny when Michael was a baby and my father was away. Reading through some of my mother's letters to him, it becomes clear that I was not a very well child as I often suffered from stomach trouble.

The local doctor looked as though he had a hollow on one side of his face, which was very scary. I remember once hiding from him and Mummy was very cross because I was not well with a usual stomach upset and a pain in my thigh.

The doctor said the pains in my stomach were possibly due to the cold weather and the pain in my thigh was rheumatism. Later there was an exchange of letters about my chapped face and hands and having to go to bed with my hands covered in oil.

Sometimes, Mummy used to take me to the beach after school while Big Granny was looking after Michael. I used to paddle in my knitted bathing costume. Once, while she sat on the stones in her coat and scarf, a man told her off and said she shouldn't let me go swimming when the sea was rough. At which my mother smiled and said 'I can't stop her.'

I had my fifth birthday at Boundstone Lane which was my first children's party - that is, the first one with guests in addition to the customary cousins and relations. My father wrote: *A children's tea party, with a ciné show, games and The Magic Fishing Rod,* a lucky dip game rigged up by him where a fishing rod which had a magnet on the end of the line could catch small gifts deep in a decorated box. He also wrote: *The great moment was the blowing out of the candles, probably J's most enjoyable party so far.*

Now, as I read his hand written notes, I know this must also reflect *his* enjoyment of his daughter's party. Could my parents' anxieties be slipping away at last? There were no more bombs falling, but daily life must have been difficult with two young children.

Food and clothing rationing and shortages of many basic household items lasted long after the war. Although I can still clearly recall my infant fears and nightmares, I now appreciate how hard my parents must have worked to shelter me from their fears and forebodings during the war.

In later years I learned that the winter of 1947 was famously hard. It was so cold the country's coal stocks froze in the depots, trains could not run and there were severe shortages. We had a lot of snow and I really wanted a sledge. I asked Daddy to make me one but he said he didn't have the time. But then I saw him tie some string to a wide flat piece of wood which I thought was a sledge, so I jumped on it and the string broke. He was cross and said it was not a sledge but to collect wood for the fire as it was so very cold and we needed to keep Michael warm.

I went for my first dental appointments early in 1947. In the Baby Book my father notes: *Quality of first teeth poor, due probably to constitution… .and first dental treatment: two fillings LH Molar, and double tooth next to it.'*

In those days, children's clothes were expensive and all the material available was natural fabric. Mrs Plunkett liked dress-making and made me a party dress out of some shiny material which had a pattern of tiny squares on it. But, when she was sewing it she cut a hole in the front by mistake. She put a little patch on it and you really could not see where the patch was but she kept saying she was sorry and how could she have.

Mrs Plunkett lived in a beautiful house in Hassocks and we walked to the front door on crunchy gravel beside long goldfish ponds covered with lily pads. She gave us buns and cakes for tea and on the table along with the jam there were jammy jars of water to catch the wasps.

Mrs Plunkett had grown up children called Desmond and Deirdre and I was surprised she didn't say Deir-dree, she said Deir-dra. Desmond flew bombers and became a war hero after being shot down and taken prisoner. He became one of the brains behind 'The Great Escape' and was reported missing for over two years.

I liked Mrs Plunkett as she was often very jolly and I think Mummy liked her a lot too because they used to giggle when they were together, especially when Michael was asleep and they thought I was too.

3

New Home, New School
1947-1949

We moved again in 1947 - far away from the South coast to the East Midlands. I was five years old - Michael was one year old. Before the war my father had worked in the offices of Permutit, a water softener company and now, on leaving the Royal Air Force, he was offered a post with the company in Nottingham. The previous incumbent - a Mr Rome - was about to retire and move. My father went ahead of us to check that the vacated house was suitable. It was, and we moved to Burleigh Road, West Bridgford.

I remember the house as being rather gloomy with lots of dark wood and a dark green kitchen. There was a garage at the side and a front and back garden.

West Bridgford and Nottingham were very different to Lancing. My mother must have missed being close to her mother and we all missed the seaside, which had been our natural playground for several years. People spoke differently; here they called each other 'duck,' which they pronounced 'dook,' or 'love,' which they pronounced 'luv,' like the 'u' in put.

If you were in a sulky uncooperative mood they said you were 'mardy' and if the weather was cold they would say 'it's a bit parky today.' Also, where I would say 'ar' they used the short 'a,' as in 'path,' 'nasty,' and 'ask.'

I heard my parents bewailing the lack of crusty rolls in the shops - all they seemed to sell were 'cobs' which were too soft. Also, what I had previously known as crumpets were called pikelets.

Sometime in the past we had acquired a black cat we called Monty - after General Montgomery - of course. Actually the entry under PETS in the Baby Book read: '*General Montgomery, July 1944, later awarded the Field Marshall's baton. Knighted 1945, decorated 1946.*' The man, not the cat.

Michael and I slept in the front bedroom. One night when Monty wanted to go out he came into our dark bedroom and sat on the table by the window and shook and wobbled it so that the dropped leaves banged against the legs.

I could not work out what it was - footsteps outside? I wondered. But footsteps wouldn't stop and start like that - or perhaps someone was trying to get in through the window or - or - what was that black shape? A ghost? And suddenly I did not care about being brave or waking up my brother or anything-

'Mummeeeeee!! I yelled.

Our mother came straight away and we solved the mystery and Monty was taken outside. She tucked me in again and kissed me goodnight. Michael had slept through everything.

A year or two later Monty died, although now I suspect he might have been put down after being run over. Our parents were worried that Michael and I would be upset, but we did not notice Monty was missing for two whole weeks. Our father said, 'He's gone to the happy hunting ground' and I wasn't quite sure what that meant but it did mean that Monty no longer crept in and sat on the table in our bedroom at night.

As my father was travelling to various companies in the East Midlands, he had a company car which was also for private use. It was a Hillman 14 and I seem to remember the registration number as KLM 381.

Daddy did some of his work at home, but was out a great deal going to different businesses. There was hardly any traffic in those days so people lucky enough to have cars would actually drive for pleasure!

One of the businesses he visited was Sketchley Dry Cleaners and another was Martin's sweet factory. Every time he went to the latter he came back with a brown paper bag full of all kinds of wrapped sweets. As sweets were still rationed, that was a real treat.

We had open fires in this house, but fuel was scarce and I have very happy memories of going wooding with my father. On these expeditions he would drive out to Clifton Village and park the car down a lane. Then we walked through the woods at the side of the river. There was a footpath and I had a great time running around the trees while Daddy picked up pieces of fallen wood to take home and dry for the fire. Fortunately the car had a large boot.

In Daddy's office room he had a filing cabinet and masses of yellow papers headed 'THE PERMUTIT COMPANY LIMITED' and also shelves of books left by Mr Rome. These were not only books relevant to the job and water softening, but quite a few novels which I read when I was older. Two I recall as being really exciting were *Black Bartlemy's Treasure* by Jeffery Farnol and *The Lancashire Witches* by William Harrison Ainsworth.

One I still have is *The Memoirs of Sherlock Holmes*, a book that always struck me as being slightly odd because the pages are set in two columns of type. Recently, a friend in the print business, explained that Sherlock Holmes stories were originally published weekly in the *Strand Magazine* and the publishers, George Newnes, had used the original magazine type setting for the book in order to save money.

I started attending the West Bridgford Preparatory school run by an elderly lady called Miss Marriot. It was was quite a long walk from home and it was there that I had an embarrassing start. The term 'Twice times' table I had previously learned in Lancing, turned out to be wrong in Nottingham.

I knew all my tables up to the twelve times, but at Miss Marriot's they said 'TWO times' and I tried very hard not to, but I kept saying 'twice' instead of 'two' and the rest of the class laughed at me.

It looked as if I did not know anything and the teacher, Miss Tomlinson, who had a jangly bracelet said I wasn't as clever as I said I was. She wore bright red lipstick and had wavy fair hair and a spiky voice. Sometimes she sat in the hut where we hung our coats and shoe bags and when she filed her nails her bracelet made a lot of noise.

No one liked her much, but really I think we were scared of her because she was good at making us jump. We also had a teacher called Mrs Watkins who had grey hair and rode a bicycle with a basket on the front. She had a loud voice and was strict, but could be very jolly, and she was always fair. I was aware my parents liked her a lot for her common sense attitude to education.

I soon settled down and became used to my new school and teachers. I remember a few of the other pupils - Geoffrey, who was a funny little boy, who said 'vace' for 'vase' and 'haitch' for 'aitch' which made us giggle, but it was not unkind laughter and he giggled too. Later, I was to move to the same road Geoffrey lived in. There was also a very pretty girl called Judith who walked as though one leg was shorter than the other.

Judith had metal braces on her legs because she had had Infantile Paralysis, a term that was in later years changed to Polio. My parents dreaded the possibility of us catching Infantile Paralysis, so we were not allowed to go anywhere crowded like swimming pools and the annual Goose Fair.

Sometimes Daddy gave me a lift to school in the car, but when he could not, Mummy used to walk me there with Michael in the pram. It was a big pram and she could put lots of shopping in it. When I was older I was allowed to go by bus and later to ride there (on the pavement) on my small two wheeler bike, which was called a fairy cycle. It was second hand, had solid wheels and was painted a lovely cream and pale blue. Until then I had owned a big tricycle which was passed on to Michael.

It must have been early in our time in Burleigh Road that my brother and I caught whooping cough. I know we were there because in the Baby Book entry for my sixth birthday under 'Those present' is written *'Mummie, Daddie, Michael (Whooping cough!)* which is the smallest party attendance in the book. I can vaguely remember I was sick every time I 'whooped' and my poor mother not only had to clear it up, but must have been beside herself with worry about Michael, who was still quite young.

I was now beginning to better understand the world about me. I enjoyed school and writing and sums and I also enjoyed drawing. I loved riding my bike and reading books, several of which were included on my birthday lists which go up to my seventh birthday.

As a toddler I was given a book of nursery rhymes and they were sung to me frequently; the words are still firmly embedded in my memory. Of the books my parents read to me, I particularly remember *Cinderella* and

Alice in Wonderland. I especially liked the song in the latter called *The Lobster Quadrille*. Several of Enid Blyton's books are also listed. These were her *First Christmas book, Holiday Book,* and especially her *Nature Lover's Book*, which I loved so much it undoubtedly contributed to my life long interest in the natural world.

I read a young children's comic called *Tiny Tots* in which the multiple syllable words were hy-phen-a-ted which I remember thinking was a bit babyish. I sometimes read a smaller comic called *Sunny Stories*. I also mention *The Children's Newspaper* in my 1948 diary. This diary was written in pencil in a thin green exercise book and covers the summer of 1948 from July to September.

Maybe it was a school task of 'What I did in the summer holidays' but there is no apparent marking of it. I wonder now if it was an idea of my father's. He always encouraged our reading and writing. He also had great ideas for making models of aeroplanes, boats, kites, and believe it or not, even of a gas works, which I painted and my father glued together for me. We played many games of football and cricket and there was a visit to the cinema where I '*saw a funny Donald Duck picture*'. We were certainly kept busy.

There are many references in the diary to my world. Ice creams do not appear to be in short supply and 'water pistles' (my spelling) featured in the hot weather towards the end of July. They were the kind which you filled by squeezing the ball shaped rubber handle, dipping the barrel into water and letting the handle slowly inflate with water.

I often had a rest in the afternoon with Mummy, no doubt when Michael had his. Michael had to go to the hospital twice - once for an X-ray and another time for some tests. I think it was to do with his ears.

My father did all his office work at home and there were always letters to be posted at the end of the day. One late afternoon :'*… I went on an errand for my Father to post some letters... .*' Other times, he and Michael came too.

That summer, I was bought the *Enid Blyton Road Safety Colouring Book* and Michael, a book about the Zoo. I had a money box which I was allowed to open the day before we went on holiday in September. Inside there was one pound and one penny. That pound would be worth more than £35 in today's money!

On our holiday in Lancing I went on the swing boats and the roundabout and to the Mermaid café and swam in the sea. I have noted the number of swims each day. Also: '*I played cricket with Peter in the after-noon*'. This is the Peter I often played with when we stayed with Big Granny. He lived with his mother in the flats opposite Big Granny's bungalow. We also went to Portsmouth where I saw '*the big ship Queen Mary and other ships....and went on the Victory*'. We went to Brighton Zoo and another day visited Mrs Plunkett, who at the time was keeping chickens.

I listed many of my daily duties of laying and clearing the table, a task which rankled even then. Not only did I have to find the pepper and salt and the correct jams or sauces for whatever meal we were having and the big serving spoons but also the knives and spoons and forks for each person AND a serviette each, in its relevant serviette ring. Obviously Michael was too young to help, but this carried on for years and it was always me that helped with the washing up and the laying and clearing of the table.

I was beginning to understand how our money worked and what the symbols:

£ s d represented: pounds shillings and pence.

In those days a *farthing* was a small brown coin with a wren on the back worth a quarter of a penny

A **halfpence** or *ha'penny* (sometimes pronounced haypney) was a bigger brown coin worth half a penny

A *penny* was the largest brown coin (bigger than the penny today)

A *threepenny bit* (sometimes pronounced thruppenny) was a small hexagonal shaped brass coloured coin worth 3 pennies

A *sixpence* was a silver coin, a bit bigger than today's 5p piece and worth 6 pennies

A *shilling* was a silver coin (a bit like a 10p coin now)

There were 12 pennies in a shilling – sometimes known as a 'bob'

There were 20 shillings in one pound £1

A *florin* was a silver coin worth 2 shillings

A *half crown* was a silver coin worth 2 shillings and six pennies

For banknotes, there was a *10 shilling note* which was brown

There was a *1 pound note* which was green.

There were also *5 pound notes* that were larger and white and only printed on one side.

So, when I was 6 how many pennies were there in a ten bob note? Work it out for yourself.

When Mummy made Christmas puddings she wrapped some very small silver coins that were ancient threepenny bits in greaseproof paper and hid them in the pudding.

If we found one in our helping we could keep it for a while then we had to give it back so Mummy could use it again the following year, but we were reimbursed!

4

'Bananas are back!'

In those days everyone was issued with ration books for food and clothing, and even I had to have my own identity card, which was finally abolished in 1952. I never heard my parents complaining about rationing and it must have been down to Mummy's thrift and home cooking skills that made it an unremarkable aspect of ours young lives.

I recall dried egg, blackcurrant purée (no jam), thick sweetened condensed milk (ugh) which Daddy ate from the tin with a spoon; home made chips, mashed potatoes, corned beef; stews and dumplings and Camp Coffee, which was a dark liquid in a bottle diluted with hot water and Daddy said tasted nothing like coffee.

Rationing lasted for fourteen years, until 1954. Today, I find it humbling when I read about the tiny amounts of meat, fats, eggs and dairy produce which were allowed per person per week. Household items like soap and washing powder were also rationed.

There were no supermarkets and ration books had to be registered with one grocer and one butcher so they could order sufficient supplies for their registered customers. Fish and poultry were not rationed, but expensive; fresh vegetables and fruit were also free from rationing but in very short supply.

One of the newsreels I remember seeing was of a young girl on the screen eating something I had never seen before. In the dark of the cinema Mummy spoke out loud saying: 'Oh lovely! Bananas are back'!

Sweets were rationed so our parents gave us each a very small amount in a twist of paper after lunch on Saturdays.

In the back garden at Burleigh Road there were lovely flowers including hollyhocks and lupins. After rain, the big soft leaves of the hollyhocks had several drips of water caught on them but the lupin leaves just had one glistening dewdrop in the middle. I used to think that was where the fairies collected their water.

My seventh birthday tea was also at Burleigh Road and there were no other relations there - just my family and several of my girl friends. Other guests were the daughters of my mother's friends, in particular Carol who became a lifelong friend. One day Mummy quietly told me that Carol had never seen her Daddy because he had been a pilot who was killed in the war.

At this stage the people in my immediate world were my mother and father, my brother Michael, school teachers and friends - including the two big boys next door called John and Roger who were very friendly. Sometimes they used to fight and we heard their mother shouting at them.

Then there was the man from the 'Pru,' who called at the house so Mummy could give him money. I did not know what it was for at the time, but later learned it was for an insurance scheme. There was also the Kleeneze man who came round selling brushes, dusters and polish.

I do not recall us having a vacuum cleaner. Rugs were taken outside and hung on a line to be beaten with a cane carpet beater. Larger carpets were brushed with a Ewbank floor sweeper.

As for washing dishes, this was all done by hand, as was the washing and drying of clothes. The water was squeezed out of clothes with a mangle, a contraption which consisted of two big horizontal rollers with a very narrow gap between them and fixed on a sturdy cast iron stand. On one side there was a big handle which turned the two rollers. The sopping wet clothes were fed through the rollers and most of the water was squeezed out into a bucket beneath.

The squeezed clothes were put into a washing basket (our baby bath) and when the weather was good, they were hung outside with pegs on a line to dry. A long piece of wood with a notch in the top called a prop was used to push the centre of the sagging line up higher so the clothes could flap in the air and not drag on the ground. Sometimes the line broke, which was a disaster.

We also had what was called a 'clothes horse' which was a wooden airer more gate shaped than modern plastic ones. It stood before the fireguard at night so the washing could dry from the heat of the dying coals.

At that time we had no television, but we frequently listened to the radio and there is an entry in my holiday diary that reads:

August 24th Tuesday

I had a comic in the morning then I had a rest on
Mother's bed with her.
I played with Michael and I had my hair washed.
I am staying up tonight to listen to Just William and
have chips for supper.

Well there's a post war treat!

That mention of *'had my hair washed'* has brought back many memories of my straight hair. It was said that hair should be brushed a hundred times every night. I did not always make the full 100. It was now quite long and every morning my mother used to plait it into two plaits, sometimes combined with two smaller ones to stop my hair escaping from above my ears. I do not remember us having a hairdryer.

If I was going to a party she would sometimes heat metal tongs on a gas ring and curl my hair into ringlets which were then divided into two bunches.

One morning I was very anxious about my homework, which was to make a chart of the month's weather. My father, wanting to help, and being a bit of a perfectionist, encouraged me to do it another way but making changes meant I had not quite finished. I stood looking at it on the dressing table and Mummy was taking ages to plait my hair.

I suddenly felt a strange buzzing in my ears and my hair was pulling and hurting. I said, 'Stop, mummy stop!' and she caught me as I collapsed and carried me to my bed calling, 'Hector! Hector!' for my father. I can remember nothing further of the episode. It was the first of the fainting episodes I have experienced throughout my life. Only recently was it diagnosed as being partly due to low blood pressure.

Well, my father's conscientiousness about my studies paid off as I received two form prizes, one *Twinkle and Winkle, Two Dormice* 1st Form prize 1948 and *The Practical Encyclopaedia for Children* 1st Form Prize

Christmas 1949, both of which I still possess.

It was also about this time that I had a confrontation with a few local peers. I had started going out on my fairy cycle, not just to school but also to the local shops. On the way I occasionally encountered a small group of children I didn't know, but they took to chasing me, especially if I was wearing a hat which I really did NOT like. It had been knitted by one of my grandmothers. I tried to avoid wearing it but my mother said I had to.

It was shaped like an old fashioned bed sock with blue and white stripes around it and a pompom on the pointy bit which hung a little way down my back. I became nervous about the combination of the hat and my bike when I saw the enemy further ahead. The inevitable happened, they ambushed me and pulled at my hat shouting things like, 'What a silly hat' and 'Ha Ha!' 'Wotcha wearing that for?'

I had to stop or I would have fallen off my bike. I called out in a loud voice, 'Stoppit! - let go of my hat!' - And they did. We then talked a bit before I carried on home. We did not become friends, but we did wave to each other. From then on I absolutely refused to wear 'that' hat, but I never told my mother the real reason why.

My father had an excellent small camera which took tiny black and white photographs that could be enlarged. He was not too keen on anyone else using it.

I must have pestered him to have a go as I was given one as a birthday present. It was larger than his camera and was box shaped. To take a picture I looked down on the view finder which was on top of the camera. The image was murky and I could only just make out the picture.

There was no zoom lens, just two settings, one for long shots beyond eight feet and a closer one for subjects at a distance of five to eight feet. (We were not yet metric) There was no flash and the film was black and white. It was called a Box Brownie and I loved it - ever since then I have owned a camera.

Unfortunately my father lost his - he thought he might have left it on the back shelf of a coach. It is the only material loss about which I remember him being really upset.

Due to the bombing, after the war there was a shortage of houses. But the government set up a limited scheme making it possible to apply for a 'new build' house. Daddy said it was a waste of time applying and we would not stand a chance. Mummy was more optimistic. She sat Michael in the pram; I walked alongside her and off we went to add our names to the list for a new house.

And we got one!

5.

Upavon
1949-1950

Can you imagine what I might have thought when our parents took my brother and me to a field on a hill and told us that this was where we were going to live? We were in the middle of a huge nowhere; the unmade road was bumpy and stony and there were no pavements.

Can I guess now what my parents were thinking at the same time? I can only suppose they were overjoyed and felt incredibly lucky. After all the traumas and doubts of wartime, the move to Nottingham had gone well; my father had a job with a car and now they could look forward to a brand new home.

I have several tiny black and white photographs of us all standing on 'our plot' in this vast wasteland. The unfinished roads had been marked out and we had a corner allocation. Later, when a school was built, the playing field was opposite our house so we kept our clear view of the city and beyond.

My memories of the house being built are few, but I do remember seeing foundations being dug and filled in and the sound of an ever churning cement mixer. I remember the scrape of the bricklayer's trowel and the brick walls growing taller each time we visited, which my brother Michael tells me, was fairly regularly. Then the scaffolding went up - wooden poles lashed together and suddenly the roof was on!

Michael and I were commandeered to endlessly squash putty between the upstairs floor boards - I presume to stop draughts. Eventually, we became bored with visits to the half built house and went to play in the garden space, which was a land of invention and adventure at the back of the house. I remember when we rigged a plank over a metal drum as a see saw. Once when I got off, at the other end Michael thudded to the ground and the plank hit my shin with such force that I had a lump on it like an egg for a week.

When completed, the house consisted of two reception rooms; a small hall and tiny cloakroom; a large kitchen with a larder; two large bedrooms and one smaller and a bathroom and separate lavatory. There was a garage at the end of the back garden and a coal shed near the house. The unmade garden lay around three sides of the house.

So, in 1949, we said goodbye to Burleigh Road. We were moving up the hill to Ellesmere Road and a new house which my parents named 'Upavon' after the home of the RAF Central Flying School. My father must have felt doubly lucky as his day job had taken him to a county where there were several small airfields and at weekends he was able to pursue his true vocation - teaching people to fly.

I recall nothing of the actual move, but I do remember my parents being very pleased with various things, for example; the parquet flooring downstairs and the orangey red floor tiles in the kitchen. However, I had the impression that they were not so impressed by the builder's skills, as the angle of the eve leaning over the bathroom meant the bath had to be sunk several inches so my father could stand up in it.

It must have been like a dream home for my mother; she had her **own new** gas stove, which she cleaned after every Sunday roast and the large kitchen was designed just as she liked it. A carpenter built cupboards everywhere with funny little push button catches.

There was a large old table in the kitchen where my mother did all her baking and food preparation and where we had our meals. It had a wide drawer where the cutlery was kept but if it was pulled out just a bit too far the drawer and its contents crashed to the tiled floor making a terrible racket.

There was no washing machine, so my mother washed and rinsed the clothes by hand in the deep butler's sink. I can remember the soap powders *Oxydol* and *Dreft* and the detergent *Tide*. My mother used to scrub really grubby collars or muddy trousers with big bars of *Fairy* soap. Sometimes she used a little 'blue bag' in the rinse to stop the whites going grey or yellowy.

Starch was a powder mixed with cold water and added to the rinsing water for certain clothes to stop them creasing too quickly. After that the sopping wet clothes went through the mangle. When the clothes were pegged out to dry, if it was windy, as it often was in our very open garden, my father's shirts puffed up with air like upside down fat men. If it was windy and frosty they stayed stiff when they were taken off the line.

We had a Hoover vacuum cleaner by then; it was an upright one and the bag had to be taken off to empty the dust into the bin. It was called a Hoover Junior.

We had no fridge, but there was a sizeable walk-in larder with a 'cold slab,' which was really just a white tiled shelf and shelves and hooks for saucepans and other kitchen clutter. A coke stove warmed the kitchen and also heated the water - allegedly - the hot water system was a topic of contention all the years we were there. We did have an electric immersion heater, but there was, according to my father, 'a fairy who keeps turning it off.'

There were two open fires, one in the front room we called the lounge and one in the back room which was known as the dining room at Christmas and the rest of the year as Daddy's office. Each of these fires had a nearby socket for a gas poker.

A fitting at one end of a rubber tube went into the socket which turned on the gas. The gas travelled through the tube and out through several holes in the metal poker. It was quickly lit with a match so there were flames coming out of the holes. Then, it was thrust under the wood and coal in the grate. After a few minutes, when the fire was burning well, the fitting was detached from the socket and the red hot poker removed from the fire to cool in the grate. The mind boggles - I cannot imagine this 'gadget' passing health and safety standards today.

A family story, often told, was once one of the sockets went wrong when there was no poker in it and gas gushed out into the room. It smelt horrible and our mother went to turn it off at the mains meter, but she couldn't budge the lever from ON to OFF.

My mother rushed into the street calling for help and fortunately a

26.

workman heard her. He managed to shift the meter lever. All the windows were opened and the dreadful smell of gas gradually went away. Michael has since told me he was the one standing in the corner with a screwdriver looking sheepish...

As we were near the top of the hill we could watch the sunsets which could be very beautiful. I also remember watching the progress of a storm as it made its way along the valley of the river Trent. I can recall several times when I found my father, the eternal pilot, upstairs staring out of the window watching the sky. When it was really bad the rain battered and splattered against the windows and the wind whistled and thumped the house. I remember the metal ventilator in our front bedroom rattling like mad, making it difficult to sleep.

When it was winter it was lovely and cosy in the lounge and kitchen if the fire and stove were lit, so long as we remembered to 'Close the door!' Upstairs it was very different. We relied on electric fires which were not turned on until we went up to get ready for bed and then turned off once we were in bed. They were not very effective when the weather was freezing cold. That was when 'Jack Frost' drew beautiful leaf patterns on the inside of the bedroom window at night while we were asleep. They never failed to amaze me when I woke up and shivered my way into my clothes. When I returned in the afternoon they had melted to a dribble of water on the window ledge.

I also remember coming home from school when I felt so freezing cold I used to run up to the bathroom where there was no heater, turn on the hot tap in the washbasin, roll up my school blouse sleeves and lower my elbows and arms into the steaming water. It was bliss.

There was no soft toilet paper in those days. We used a brand called 'Bronco' and the paper was very scratchy. It had printed in green capital letters: MEDICATED WITH IZAL GERMICIDE, on each sheet.

We did eventually acquire a bathroom heater, but the lavatory was separate and that was always freezing cold and draughty. In the winter no one stayed in there very long. It was next to the bathroom at the gloomy end of a short corridor. In the dark evenings I used to push the cistern handle down, turn the light out and then run like mad to get to the top of the lit stairs, before the water flushed.

I was not really scared of anything but it was a bit creepy - then it became a game. In later years I found out that Michael had done exactly the same thing.

***

So there we were - happily ensconced in our new home. However it seems my brother and I did not always enjoy the best of health. According to my diary, which I wrote in the summer before we moved, there are several mentions of my brother having to go to the Children's Hospital for tests of some kind. He had chronic earache and I constantly suffered from tonsillitis.

I used to run a temperature and had the most ghastly sore throats. Once, I could not eat and it seemed to go on forever. When I began to feel a bit better, my mother, trying to tempt me to eat something, brought me some gently cooked fried bread. It was not in the least bit crisp, just warm and salty tasting and - delicious!

My mother ended up being commanded to bring me three more slices, one at a time, up and down the stairs. I have never forgotten that taste and never tasted it since. It would have been cooked in lard; in those days butter was rationed and olive oil was a character in Popeye. But it could be bought in tiny bottles at the chemist.

These ear and throat ailments must have come to a head (sorry) and in early January 1950, Michael and I went into the Convent Nursing Home; Michael to have both adenoids and tonsils removed and me, just my tonsils.

Some of this I can remember. We were in a large high ceilinged room, all of which was painted brown. I was disgusted and upset because they put me in a big cot - I was eight years OLD for goodness sake! Michael was about to be four, so of course he was in a cot. There was another cot in the room which remained empty but on the other side of the room there was a bed with an older girl in it who wailed and moaned all the time.

She was called Dorothy and had had her appendix removed. Sometimes she pressed the bell and the nuns would come running in and pull the

28.

curtains round her bed. There were no curtains round our cots. Michael and I had both taken small bags of our special things with us but they were taken away for a while - maybe because there were some edible items in them.

We must have been in the nursing home for several days because there was time for our parents to send us get well cards and for me to reply. In my letter I write 'I am quite good friends with Dorothy now.' As she recovered we used to chat across the room.

At home, Michael and I were sharing the same bedroom - the large one with the rattling ventilator at the front of the house. Michael clearly re-members our parents saying we had squeaky voices when we returned from the nursing home. We were even allowed to have the electric fire on all day.

Our stay in hospital must have been a major event for our parents. Even when I was mad about sleeping in a cot I noticed that my mother was very upset to leave us in the nursing home. They must have been so relieved to have us safely home and recovering.

Antibiotics were not readily available then and there was no vaccine for polio until 1955. Later on, I remember Michael contracting Scarlet Fever. I was not sharing the bedroom with him by then and I was very impressed by the great hoo-ha about fumigating the room and disinfecting all his bedclothes.

Unless we had fairly critical symptoms we rarely went to the doctor's surgery. Mummy regularly dosed us up with home medications like *Haliborange*, which was a fish oil supplement with vitamins A & D: *Minadex* - a tonic of vitamin and mineral supplements for children and adults, especially after illness; *Syrup of Figs* for constipation and Andrews Liver Salts which my father took often. *Lucozade* was more like a treat after you were ill. When they had a headache my parents took Aspirin, the only pain killer obtainable at the chemist shop.

I frequently had dreams about being chased by tigers or lions. I also dreamed of being able to fly. I would simply 'pedal' and rise off the ground - gently pedalling all the time - rising up into the clouds.

6.

Toeing the line

At some point in 1950 I remember my father taking me to a school in a huge old house on the far side of the city. A very nice lady asked me to do some writing and sums. She also asked me some questions. This was a test for a place at the Nottingham Girls High School. I did well enough to secure a place in Form 2, starting in the September. I know my father was really pleased. I always remember him as being very keen on our education, constantly encouraging us to read and write and to do things 'properly'.

It must have been the influence of his RAF days; he could not bear 'sloppiness' which included the way Americans saluted, or stood with their hands in their pockets, saying 'OK'. His other dislikes were: jeans, chewing gum, and the word 'got,' which, he said should be replaced by another verb as often as possible. Similarly he disliked the use of the word 'nice' and said we should always look for something more suitable. To this day his rules still echo in my head whenever I write.

As I understand more, I realised that these rules were a simple demonstration of my father's love of the English language. He could also show us how to have fun with words and wrote an acrostic for me just before my eighth birthday:

Just a line on your tome
Underneath all the others
Don't laugh at my poem
(It may be my Mother's)!

Tho' I'm fond of the pig
Horse and elephant too,
The squeak of a mouse
Appals me anew!

Yes, blue and green sweets
Love I with great zest
Or the bird as he tweets
Round the edge of his nest

I've finished my verse in a style full of piffle
Though I've used many words I've said very little!
(In case you haven't noticed, the first letter of each line spells my name)

He was a stickler for punctuality and I know I transgressed several times as he made me write lines. I still have one set that I wrote which he has dated 20.3.50. He dated everything. I was only eight!

They are written on his plain yellow office notepaper and not only had I to write, 'I must remember the time' twenty times but I had to draw the lines on the paper as well. I seemed to have got away with only nineteen as I had not left enough spaces for twenty.

Another time it was, 'I must be punctual' and I remember being so furious with him that I tried to spell 'punctual' in as many different ways as I could but soon realised there were not enough letters in it to make it worthwhile. Now I am on time for everything and become anxious if I think I might be late. However it must be partly genetic as my Irish Granny (father's mother) was a total neurotic about time and would insist he drove her to the station far too early to catch a train. I was once with them when we arrived on the platform so early that we saw the previous train pulling out and she thought she had missed the one she had planned to catch.

I do not recall my brothers having to write lines. Ever. Michael says he did but he cannot remember what they were.

My father had been christened into the Catholic Church in Meerut in India, where my grandfather was serving in the British Army and he was brought up in the same religion for all his childhood. In his mother's diary she wrote that he was confirmed when they were stationed in Abbassia, Cairo, in Egypt and was also an altar boy when he was nine years old.

I heard my mother once say something about 'High Church', but at some point my father parted from Catholicism. So, my brothers and I were christened in the Church of England. Although he had not insisted we become Catholics he was always keen for us to go to Sunday school. Before the move to our new house I attended the Sunday School at the Methodist Church in West Bridgford and I have kept a rather tattered programme. Later we sometimes went to St Giles for a short family Church of England service on Sunday mornings. Once or twice he insisted we all went to part of the Good Friday service, which I hated because it was so utterly dreary and boring. After we moved to Upavon, the Sunday School and church I attended was in Edwalton, a village about a mile out of West Bridgford.

At home, we always said grace before each meal: 'For what we are about to receive may the Lord make us truly thankful. ' There was also a longer one which we also used at my first school in Lancing:

Thank you for the food we eat
Thank you for the world so sweet
Thank you for the birds that sing
Thank you God for everything

Sometimes we muddled the first and second lines so that we were eating the world and the food was 'so sweet' and then we got the giggles.

Father was also strict about table manners: no elbows on the table, sit up straight, chew with your mouth closed, never talk with your mouth full, or put your knife in your mouth and always finish what is on your plate.

The last could be really difficult and sometimes Michael just could not eat all of his cabbage. Our father who must have seen some terrible deprivation abroad in his boyhood years came out with his usual line: 'Think of the starving children in India.' Once, when Michael was older, he suggested father sent the cabbage to India and there was a sudden hush around the table. Fortunately, father laughed.

Yes, father was a disciplinarian, and I think I received the sharper end of his views, as I have no recollection of my brothers having to write lines or help with the washing up. Despite my occasional bursts of 'It's not fair!' I was having a good time in the new house with my little brother and getting to know some new friends who lived down the road where the older houses were.

We had such amazing freedom in those days. The school, Jesse Gray, was being built, but it was well away from where we lived, so the lorries seldom passed our house. There was very little traffic and it took a while for the plots close to us to be built upon. The one next to our back garden was virtually the last. There were unmade roads all around us and no nearby bus route for ages. Cars rarely drove past and the only vehicles were the occasional lorries belonging to the builders.

During the day there was often the churning sound of a cement mixer, which was not very loud once it had clattered and chugged into action. At weekends a light aircraft might fly over and we used to wave to it in case it was dad. A grumpy milkman called daily and we had a weekly delivery of groceries.

How quiet it was. One hot summer evening, lying in bed with my bedroom window open, I could hear the wind gently hissing as it blew through the barley in the field next to us. Sometimes a wind preceded a brief storm with dark skies and rain and lightning and thunder. However that hot evening there was no storm and I fell asleep to the quiet shshshing sound outside my window.

***

At first I did not wander far from home. Watching the school being built was interesting enough, especially when a boy had his wellington boot sucked off his foot into a giant mound of sticky mud. A workman recovered it for him but the boy did not seem too pleased - when he looked inside it he said 'Ugher.' He would not put his foot in it and went away limping on one boot.

To have fields around our home was a new experience and I now had a bigger bike, a black sit up-and-beg Hercules with almost full size wheels. I rode around the bumpy roads with little chance of colliding with a car. I made friends with two sisters, Katherine and Alison - one was older and the

33.

other younger than me. They both had hair that almost came to their shoulders. Katherine was the more serious while Alison was more of a joker and inclined to be accident prone.

They were Scottish and lived at the far end of our road. We used to play hopscotch together as they had a pavement outside their house. Their Irish terrier, Paddy, was a sandy sort of colour. They also had a hen coop in their garden which after the war had been cleaned and painted inside as a play-house. It was about two feet off the ground and if we climbed up the little ladder and went in we were told not to jump around but sit quietly as their parents were worried the floor would go through.

I remember their mother had dark curly hair and always walked very briskly with her heels making a quick click clock sound on the pavement. She had a strong Scottish accent which made her sound cross. Their father was bald and smoked a pipe. They went to Dundee or Aberdeen for their holidays.

We often played dressing up and putting on shows and we persuaded other children in the road join in. There was also a family called Knight who owned a greengrocers shop in West Bridgford where in later years I had a holiday job.

I became friends with the eldest daughter Sheila. She had dark hair and was pretty with red cheeks and always good fun. She had a brother Dennis and a little sister Brenda who, with her mother's encouragement, was always hanging on to us. They were all a bit plump. One morning when I called earlier than usual for Sheila to come out to play, I was amazed to see they were eating cake for breakfast! Not just one cake, but there were several to choose from in different tins on the table. They used to go sailing on the river Trent at Beeston and on several occasions were kind enough to take me too.

I learned a lot about sails and ropes (sheets) and tacking. Sometimes the boys swam in the river and I tried it once but I did not like the feel of the mud under my feet. It felt soft and slimy - not anything like the firm sand or pebbles I was used to when swimming in the sea at Lancing. Sheila eventually moved to New Zealand and we are still in touch.

Then there was David who lived with his granny and granddad across the road. We never thought to question where his parents were. David had brown hair and was often smiling. He was very polite to my parents and a good friend to me. Occasionally - but memorably - his grandparents would drive David and me to a farm where we collected chicken and duck eggs and we picked blackberries from the hedgerows. David is in some of my very old photographs.

There was another family with two sons - the younger one was Geoffrey who I had already met at Miss Marriot's. Later they had a pretty little sister, Jane, who had curly hair. We rarely went into their house and I think it was because it smelled peculiar, but even though I am sure we all noticed it, we never ever talked about it.

Mrs Mee lived across the road and over the years became a good friend to my mother. Mr Mee was related to Arthur Mee, who started the *Children's Newspaper*. They had a lovely garden with a stream and goldfish. Mr Mee was always grumpy but Mrs Mee was very friendly - especially when their grandson Ian came to stay in the holidays. Ian had very fair hair and was quite shy until he got to know us all. He was really good at drawing and colouring in and always kept inside the lines which I could never do. His colouring always looked lovely and smooth and neat and mine was always scribbly. Later, Ian became a graphic designer.

That first summer at Upavon must have been special for all of us. The open land around was constantly changing; crops were being harvested, there were trees to climb, and there were wastelands of long grass where we played hide and seek and stalked crickets and grasshoppers. The natural world was on our doorstep with chirping birds, scatterings of wild flowers and masses of bugs and caterpillars to discover.

I still used *Enid Blyton's Nature Lover's Book* and also, *The Observer's Book of Wild Flowers*. I often used to press a flower with its leaves between blotting paper, gently placing them between pages in a book at the bottom of a heavy pile. The trouble was I often forgot how many flowers I had put in the book and they would fall out, sometimes more than a year later if I read the book again.

We went back to Lancing for our holiday and I was so happy to see the sea and to go swimming and paddling and building castles again. I also met my friend Peter again who I often played with when I was staying at Big Granny's. He was very good fun and really accomplished at sums. This may have been the last time I saw him. Later I heard he had written maths text books and when I had a temporary job at the Institute of Physics his name popped up on the membership card files. There was an address but I never followed it up. I was too occupied by being pregnant with my first baby.

I always felt sad to leave the sea to go back to Nottingham, but I had usually stopped crying by the time we drove through Worthing. There were no motorways then. However, that Autumn, there was excitement ahead. Mummy was going to have another baby and I was going to start at the Nottingham Girls High School.

Form 2
September 1950 – September 1951

There was much to do and buy before I started at the Nottingham Girls High School. Well, not so much that I had to do and buy, the tasks fell on my pregnant mother. I needed a new school uniform which had to be bought from a special uniform shop called Dixon & Parkers on Friar Lane in Nottingham.

The school uniform covered a huge array of specific items. There was a navy blue blazer, tie, mackintosh and beret. The winter coat was a lighter blue tweed. Our long sleeved blouses were a saxe blue and the skirts, tunics and divided skirts, called shorts for games, were a darker blue - a muddy sort of blue between the blue of the blouses and navy blue.

To carry money we had to have either a purse on a shoulder strap or a purse belt, which I had. Mine was navy blue and fastened at the front with a big clasp and had a purse with a zip fastener sewn into the waistband.

Cardigans were blue or fawn and knee length socks were fawn. We could wear white socks in summer. The summer dresses were in pale blue, pale green or a peachy pink colour - all in a small check.

Whenever a pupil was out and about in school uniform, a badge for the school had to be shown, on the blazer pocket or the beret. The badge design was pale blue on navy, with the letters NGHS and an owl motif. The beret badge had to be sewn on as well as name tapes on everything.

For games and gym we wore short sleeved blue aertex shirts with baggy navy blue over-knickers for gym. These gym knickers had to have our names embroidered on them at a size legible from a distance. Undoubtedly that was for instant recognition by the gym teacher if we looked as if we were going to try some dangerous manoeuvre, but would not be much use if we were hanging upside down.

Our names also had to be embroidered on the front of our art overalls.

We had to have gym bags with our names on them and plimsolls, a satchel and a variety of pencils, crayons and a rubber and a ruler.

As the school was on the other side of the city, my journey meant catching two buses and some walking. Luckily for me, my neighbourhood friends, Katherine and Alison, were also going there and their father gave me a lift with them every morning, but I had to make my own way home. Katherine and Alison's satchels were 'different'; they were worn high on the back with two straps - like a rucksack. I think they were Scottish satchels.

So in September 1950, there I was on my first day at 'big' school, looking very new. The school turned out not to be just the one big Victorian house I had first visited, but four in a row on Arboretum Street. However the first year of my school life was spent in a classroom on the opposite side of the road to the main school.

It was made of some prefabricated material and was known as The Hut. Behind it there was a piece of grassed land called the Little Field where we had morning playtime and played rounders.

The original school buildings were divided into A, B, C and D blocks and consisted of many classrooms that were of different shapes and sizes due to the original design of the houses. These rooms were for the Lower 3rds up to the second year 6th form. There was a kindergarten or prep school at the D end, but my Form 2 seemed to be in a separate limbo land, probably to avoid overcrowding in the main buildings.

Within this confusing conglomeration of rooms and floors there was also a gym, science labs, art rooms and the Hall.

The gym was purpose built with one long side on Arboretum Street. Although there were thickly frosted glass windows up to quite a high level, we could just see outside if we climbed to the top of a rope. The gym also doubled as an exam room.

There were two laboratories, a Chemistry lab, which was on the ground floor off the Covered Way and a Physics and Biology Lab, which had tiered seats and was on the first floor of A block. There were two art rooms - one very large studio on the second floor of A Block and another smaller one which was on the top floor of B Block.

I remember very little of that first day. We must have had to cross the road to the Hall in the main building for morning Assembly, where there were several hundred other girls. We sat on the floor and our class was at the front, very close to the stage on which the 6th formers, prefects and head girl sat on chairs facing us and the rest of the school.

The teachers sat on chairs down the side of the room, next to their classes. Suddenly everyone stood up and went quiet when the Headmistress, Miss Milford, came in. She wore an academic gown for Assembly and was quite tall. Her grey hair was tied back in a low bun. She stood in the middle of the stage and said, 'Good morning school' and we all said, 'Good morning Miss Milford'. We sang a hymn and then one of the girls on the stage read a passage from the Bible and we had a prayer. We sat down again and some pupils who did not attend assembly came in. At first I thought they were all latecomers but later someone told me that some of them were of other religions.

Miss Milford read out some of the notices, the first of which was to welcome the new girls and the second was to remind us not to run down the Covered Way which linked all the houses. This reminder was a frequent notice. For a while, I thought it was the 'Cupboard Way' until someone put me right.

My memory of my first year is rather hazy, but some things registered. We often wrote with a pencil in our exercise books but I also began writing with a pen dipped in ink in my first English composition book. Our desks were wooden and each had a lid over a space to store books. On the right hand side at the front there was a hole holding a small ceramic inkwell.

Being left-handed it was more difficult to reach the inkwell on the right side, which meant I had to stretch across my work to dip my pen nib in the ink and sometimes the ink dripped and stained my fingers.

I still have my brown covered exercise book for English Composition which gives some clearer indication of what was going on in my first year. The first essay is about Black Beauty and another was about the 75th anniversary of the founding of the school, with an account of the church service we all attended. On October 11th there is an essay about Goose Fair and it is written in some detail.

Among many other topics there is evidence of studying the following poems: *The Jumblies, The Owl and the Pussy Cat, The King's Breakfast, The Scarecrow* and *From a Railway Carriage*. There are also references to *Ali Baba* and *Sinbad*, the correct layout of letters, imaginative writing on the basis of a story we had been told, a vocabulary test, how to write a scene from a play, an essay on spring cleaning, a dictation, which we wrote in ink with those awful relief nib dip pens and the story of *The Selfish Giant*, in which we were asked to underline verbs in red and nouns in green, a first test in parsing. There is a spelling list on the back page where I had to write out three times the correct versions of the words I had originally spelled incorrectly.

One of the most interesting essays to me is dated October 4th 1950. It was written in pencil and includes all my spelling mistakes and sentence structure:

```
                       How I Get Home
                     October 4th 1950


When I get out of school I first of all walk up
Abouretum Street, and then up Addisson Street.  Then,
I walk along Forest Road until I get to Mansfield
Road.  I cross there, and then walk down to the
nearest bus stop, and wait until a trolley bus or a
motor-bus with City on it comes.  I stay on until it
comes to the terminus and then I get off.  I cross the
square and wait for a number eleven motor-bus on the
road opposite Long Row.  Then I get on and wait and
get off at the terminus, which is Valley Road. I wait
until the bus turns back because it is a dangerous
corner, and then cross, then, I walk strait up and
over the railway bridge and turn right then I walk on
and the first turning on the left and that is my road
and my house is on the corner of the first turning on
the right because it is a corner house.
```

It was marked with a √ and Quite good in red ink

What I did not mention, was that on Forest Road there was a sweet shop and a stamp shop. I collected stamps and often looked in the shop window and sometimes went in to buy some. The square in Nottingham town centre was officially known as the Old Market Square.

At Valley Road terminus I got off the bus on what was then a fairly quiet Melton Road. Because the bus obscured approaching traffic I was forbidden to cross until it had reversed, what I call 'turns back', into Valley Road to make its return journey.

This essay was followed by a map, also in pencil, of my walk home from Valley Road. The whole journey must have taken me at least an hour. Only two months later, in December 1950, I was going to be nine years old.

I also had half an hour of homework each night and an hour at the week-end.

***

Soon after I started at the high school, mother had my brother Robert. My long days away at school meant I did not see much of him during the week but at weekends I became familiar with the new baby routine. I remember him as being a big, blonde, jolly baby who became a loved member of the family.

Looking back, it must have been a very hard time for my mother, who had to cope with everyone else's routines and also bring up a new baby. Over the years, to lighten the housework load, she had various cleaners who came once a week.

The one I particularly remember was May, who I thought was one of the most hideous human beings I had ever seen. She was almost hunchbacked, had sparse lank black hair and a ruddy face with a mouth which always looked very wet. Every mid morning when she came, May sat at the kitchen table talking in a broad Nottingham accent, drinking tea and dribbling while she ate mother's home made cake.

She lived in the Meadows, then one of the most deprived areas of Nottingham. Mummy used to give her food and sometimes clothes to take home. After Robert was born we also had a Home Help who came in to be just that - but I do not think the she did much cleaning - probably ironing and washing - all those nappies again!

My parents were very surprised to hear the Home Help had a television because they could not, or rather they chose not to afford one. Our father did not want us to have a television because he said it would distract us from our homework.

Later on he did rent one 'just for the school holidays' and in his later years - I could hardly believe it until I saw it - there were TWO in the house, one in the lounge for mother, who enjoyed watching the snooker and one in his room where he dozed watching it and then fell fast asleep.

So, we may not have had a television then, but we did listen to the wireless. *Children's Hour* was on the Home service between five and six o'clock. The series I particularly remember were *Toytown, Ballet Shoes, The Swish of the Curtain, Norman and Henry Bones*, (a boy detective series), *Jennings at School*, and *Winnie the Pooh*. There was a presenter whose voice I can clearly remember; he was known as Uncle Mac and at the end of *Children's Hour* he said, 'Goodnight Children, everywhere.'

At lunchtime there was also *Listen with Mother* which was for little children with songs and a story. Then in the evenings on the Light Prgramme there were drama series such as *Dick Barton, Special Agent, Paul Temple* and *Riders of the Range*, I also remember enjoying *Top of the Form*, a quiz programme which later went on to television.

Then, of course, there was homework to do but what else did I do with my time at home? Well, I saw my local friends; we played in each others' houses or went out into the fields and climbed trees and played hide and seek and collected wild flowers. We also rode our bikes. We played marbles and five stones or jacks, known as Snobs in Nottingham. We also had whips and tops which could be very frustrating when the tops kept falling over.

When we stayed indoors because of the weather, we might dress up and act out stories or just dance around to the wind up gramophone, We played simple card games like Snap or Beat your Neighbour out of Doors or Happy Families if someone had the necessary pack. There was Pick-up-Sticks, a nerve testing game played with twenty-five thin pointy coloured sticks about

12 inches/20cms long. First, you held all the sticks in bunch, upright on a table or the floor. Then you let them fall and they ended up in a muddled pile. Each colour represented a different score and the game was to try and 'pick up' as many sticks as possible without causing any others to move or wobble. It could be really tricky.

For a time there was a craze for Cowboys and Indians, which involved dressing up and hiding behind furniture and shooting each other with cap guns and yelling a lot. There were also banging rockets which were about 12cm long. A cap was loaded in the removable nose end and the rocket was thrown up in the air and so long as it landed nose first, made a loud bang. We were not supposed to use them indoors but they would not work on carpets anyway.

On Sundays I used to go to Sunday school and I also remember fancy dress competitions at the church fêtes. Once, my almost winning outfit consisted of my bathing costume over which I wore a raffia skirt (mother's invention) and garlands and anklets of paper flowers. I wore my hair down (no plaits, hooray!) with a coronet of more flowers. I was a Hawaiian girl.

We all had to parade around the vicarage garden in front of the judges and I received a lot of applause, but I was pipped at the post by a tall gangly boy dressed as a sugar cube. He wore white tights and a white jumper with long sleeves and his head and shoulders were inside a huge white square box with 'Tate and Lyle' on the sides. I did not mind coming second as I thought his costume was brilliant!

I also enjoyed making things. I made woollen balls or pompoms by winding wool round two circles of card with a ring cut out of the middle. There was also a craze for 'French Knitting' which involved a cotton reel with four pins at the top round which wool was wound and slipped over to produce a snake of knitted wool that could be sewn together to make - anything!

Sometimes I messed around with plasticine, making snakes and worms or trees with little bowl shaped nests with tiny plasticine eggs in them. I still love the smell of plasticine.

At one time I had two plaster caste sets, one of Christmas characters

43.

the other of farm animals. There was a red rubbery mould for each character and to make a model I first mixed some 'Plaster of Paris' powder with water and filled the mould with the plaster mixture. Next I fixed the neck of the mould in a cardboard holder and hung it upside down over a bowl or jug until the plaster had set. Then I had to carefully peel off of the mould and if the model looked all right I could paint it with poster paint.

This was all done on a tray on our big kitchen table. I soon learned about the differing qualities of 'Plaster of Paris'. The dental one was white and although it took longer to set, it had a better painting surface. The other which I think was called commercial 'Plaster of Paris' was pale pink and set almost too quickly - as I found out when I once left some in the mixing bowl too long.

There were about five moulds in each set but it became rather boring to make the same Father Christmas each year and the cockerel's head often got stuck behind in the mould as the neck was very thin.

I also enjoyed making models of places like a village or zoo or farm. Each started off with a base made of a large flat piece of strong cardboard. I painted this with whatever I imagined the model needed - fields, roads, ponds and rivers. Then I made paper and card models of houses, shops, sheds, barns, fences, and trees and stuck them on to the base. Actually it was not always necessary to stick them down - sometimes it was more fun to move them round and change the layout of the model.

For a while I had been collecting shop bought models of tiny people, tractors, and animals, to go on to a model and if there was anything missing I tried to make them. This could be tricky as a home-made paper model of a mouse could end up being bigger than a shop bought cow. The plaster cast farm animals were also far too big as when placed in the farm yard they looked like a giant alien species.

These activities all involved the use of glues of various kinds. I particularly remember *Gloy*, which was a white opaque glue and came in a big pot shaped like a round flat topped pyramid with the brush attached to the lid. Then there was another goldenish glue which looked like syrup and it came in a smaller bottle with a pointy red rubber top in which you had to cut a little slit so the glue came out when it was pressed on to a surface to be attached. There was also *Copydex*, a runny white glue; *GripFix*, also white, but much stiffer. It came in a little tub with a plastic applicator. Airfix glue came in a tube and was used to stick balsa wood together, as in aeroplane kits, and which dried very quickly.

I was also given a book called *Hundreds of Things a Girl Can Make* which was simply that, and I made quite a few of them, for example the woollen pom poms I mentioned earlier, a handkerchief doll (no paper tissues in those days), and how to dry flowers.

Michael and baby Robert took up much of our mother's time but I was rarely banned from the kitchen table with my messy activities. My mother must have been very patient and I was never bored.

8

Out of School

Most of all I loved books and I read whenever I could. It is about this time I discovered Enid Blyton and was enthralled by the *Famous Five* books and the Adventure series. I read quickly, as was proved when I was invited to a friend's birthday party. That Saturday morning I bought her a present of an Enid Blyton book I had not previously read. I managed to read it with just enough time left to wrap it, have lunch and go to the party.

I also liked comics. *The Beano* and the *Dandy* were fun to read, with characters such as the Bash Street Kids, Desperate Dan, Dennis the Menace, Korky the cat and Pansy Potter. These were produced in faraway Dundee by a company called DC Thomson.

Then a new comic came out, more like a magazine for children, called *Eagle* which had a much shinier look and carried a comic strip of the main hero Dan Dare on the front page. Soon after, *Girl* followed, which was like a sister to the *Eagle*. We had the *Eagle* and *Girl* delivered each week and it was always a treat when they came through the letterbox.

The next major event in my life was in the summer of 1951. My father drove Roger, from Burleigh Road, and me down to London to visit the Festival of Britain. We left very early in the morning and I remember sliding around on the big leather seat at the back - no seatbelts then or motorways for that matter.

Parking was no problem and there were no parking meters in those days. I remember names of things like the Dome of Discovery, which was filled with exhibits and the Skylon, which was just a pylon that pointed up into the sky. I remember very little of what we did there, except that we sat on a very cold stone wall when we had our picnic lunch. However, I do remember the drive back and how exciting it was when it was dark and I could watch the town lights whizzing by until I slept.

Meanwhile, back at Upavon the roads near us had been surfaced and new grass was slowly covering the school field. Michael had started at West Bridgford Prep and Robert was very lively. The garden needed attention and I enjoyed working in it. My parents paid me sixpence an hour to dig and hoe the heavy soil but at some later stage they engaged Bill to help. Bill was the epitome of the term 'gentle giant'. He was tall and very strong. He didn't talk much, but he seemed kind. Knowing my father's affiliation to the services it is likely that he was a demobbed soldier.

A green privet hedge was planted down the length of the back garden and a golden one at the front. We had rose bushes in a small bed in the front garden. There was a well-known rose grower called Harry Wheatcroft close by, further down the Melton Road from Edwalton, and I went there with my parents to buy some rose plants.

My memory mainly consists of going into a little office where a man sat eating strong smelling kippers with his fingers. My parents must have ordered the roses, but when we left my mother whispered comments on the state of the man's hands and whether he had washed them before eating the kippers.

Another feature of the front garden was a hydrangea by one of the front gates. Mother used to sometimes tip used tea leaves on the roots to make the colour darker.

At first there were several seasons of growing potatoes which were supposed to be good for breaking up the clay soil. Some young trees were planted along the road side of the back garden. They were meant to be a wind shield but seemed to take ages to grow tall enough to be effective.

Eventually a lawn was laid at the back and a smaller one at the front. There was a time when we had fruit bushes of black currants, red currants and gooseberries. Mother used to make delicious pies and crumbles. I also remember clumps of chrysanthemums and tall Michaelmas daisies and a couple of small apple trees and a plum tree which were quite productive after a few seasons.

Neither of my parents were ardent gardeners; my mother had very little spare time, but father used to mow the lawns when necessary with a mechanical lawnmower. It was pretty hard work, I know, as occasionally I was allowed to have a go. Michael and I were sometimes commandeered to do an hour of weeding or stoning which were the most tedious garden activities ever.

One year, when I was much older, I offered to prune the trees and Michael helped me. He was not totally dedicated to the task and instead of dumping all the pruned branches to make a bonfire he stuck several of them into part of the front lawn and a flower bed at the side of the house.

These surprisingly took root and the following year we realised what had happened and quickly pulled them up. If we had thought more, we could have had a small orchard of plum trees but I am not sure our parents would have approved.

By now my wardrobe consisted of my new school uniform, one set of 'best' clothes - for church and going out; a dress for parties, and one set of play clothes. I wore Clark's sandals in the summer and lace up shoes or wellington boots in the winter.

Our mother was very particular about shoes - well she had been a dancer and when trying on a new pair we had to stand with our feet under a machine which showed an x-ray of the new shoes with our feet inside them. We could look down through a viewer to see a murky green image of our feet wiggling within the outline of the new shoes. Our mother and the shop assistant looked down two other side viewers to see if the shoes were a good fit. These machines were withdrawn in the 70's for fear of negative effects from the rays.

Once a new pair was purchased that was not the end of it because mother then took the shoes to a cobbler to ask for raised insteps to be inserted to keep our foot arches properly supported.

Talking of shoes and feet, I had been given some roller skates, either as a birthday or Christmas present. They were very slow as they were only single ball bearings with no rubber on the wheels and they made a terrible noise. Because of the racket they made, once, when I was on my own, I was attacked by the local scary dog - an Alsatian called Dusty who we always avoided.

He must have been confused by the noise my feet were making and I

48.

ended up back pedalling with my skates until I was wedged against a fence with the terrifying dog's forepaws on my shoulders. His gaping, panting wet jowl and lolling tongue stuck right in my face! I remember saying faintly 'Down, Dusty, down, good boy' for ages and he must have got the message eventually but I returned home a gibbering wreck and have not liked dogs ever since..

New best or play clothes were a special event and one Saturday morning mother and I went up town to buy me a new outfit. After a lot of humming and haaing I was the proud owner of a new green and beige tweed skirt and a green zip up jacket, not unlike today's anoraks, but called a windcheater then. This jacket had a collar that could stand up, pockets and a gathered elastic waist with six inches or more of length below.

I was so happy with it that the moment we were home I put it on and rushed out to play on my roller skates. My friends were nowhere to be found so I consoled myself by messing about on our garden path, sitting on an old metal tray on my skates and - horror of horrors - I caught my new jacket in the wheels. They made two neat little vertical rips in the back below the waistline. I was very upset and rushed in howling. My mother was very understanding and after comforting me made an as good - as -invisible mend.

Later I was given double ball bearing skates, which were quieter; they hummed along and I could achieve much more speed. I became quite good at dancing in them, well, gliding round in circles. I tried skating in the school playground across the road but the surface was too rough. The outdoor rink in the Peter Pan fairground on the seafront in Brighton was much better.

I had another confrontation with my peers, this time on the walk back home from the bus stop on Valley Road. A nearby boys' school, Grosvenor House, finished their day just after I crossed the main road and started walking along Boundary Road towards the railway bridge.

Two small boys appeared and started chasing me. In their yellow and black striped uniform they had the same look and nuisance value as wasps. I decided to run too so they didn't catch up with me. This happened a few

49.

times and one day they became more raucous and I suddenly felt scared of them. When I arrived home that afternoon I told mother and she said, 'What do you think they are going to do to you?' and I said I did not know and went upstairs to change, thinking she just did not care.

The next day, they started running and I decided I would walk normally. I felt a bit wobbly, but when they caught up with me I turned and said, 'WHAT do you WANT?' as loudly and sternly as I could (good old Elocution lessons!). They looked blank for a moment and then collapsed into giggles and said they did not know.

The tension gone, we had a short conversation about the schools we went to and our names until I turned the corner. From then on we used to talk to each other, if they ran to catch me up. However, I did not walk that way home for much longer. I changed to the 24 bus, which now the road was made up, at last came to the top of the hill, much nearer to our house.

At this time, I began going out with my parents to search for a flat or house close by for my father's parents. I remember how we did not bother to look inside places which had a clear line in the outer brickwork showing where the flood came up to in 1947. Some of them must have been flooded to a depth of several feet.

It was later in the 50's when there were special flood defences put into action, and among other measures, the River Trent was widened. Concrete steps were created all the way from the Clifton Suspension Bridge to Trent Bridge and beyond.

I have a memory of one winter, when I was older, going with friends down the hill and walking towards the river which had burst its banks. The flood water had spread over the fields and frozen hard. It was a beautiful crisp day and frosty hedges rose well above the surface of the ice. The water below cannot have been any deeper than about two feet. We had a fantastic time pretending to ice skate in our wellingtons and screaming with laughter when someone fell over.

There were people there on ice skates and they looked so elegant as they moved across the ice. It made me think of a children's picture book which had illustrations of people skating in the countryside in the 'old days'.

9

Holidays

When I was young we went back to Lancing every year for our summer holiday and stayed near Big Granny. There were no motorways and the journey by car from Nottingham took us all day. Sometimes we stopped for a snack in London at Lyons Corner House near Marble Arch, having parked in the Edgware Road, which was free of traffic meters in those days.

The restaurant, down a wide staircase, was huge and there were uniformed waitresses know as 'Nippies' to take our order. It was always busy with people sitting at crowded tables, eating and chatting. Once there was a trio of musicians wandering round the tables. One was playing a piano accordion and singing jolly songs in a foreign language. I prayed they would not come to our table, but they did and they were very loud and kept smiling at us. My parents laughed and clapped them but I felt very embarrassed.

I have in my mind it was 126 ½ miles from Nottingham to Lancing. We passed the time singing songs like *Keep Right on to the End of the Road* and *Pack up your Troubles* and nursery rhymes for Michael. We played games like I Spy with my little Eye. Sometimes to make it easier, we would use a colour instead of a letter of the Alphabet. When the *I Spy* books came out they helped to make the journey go more quickly. These were small books which cost sixpence each and had titles like: *I Spy Cars*, *I Spy at the Seaside*, *I Spy Dogs*. Inside there were pictures of things to 'Spy' which you ticked off when you saw them.

After London I knew we were getting close to Lancing because the road near the Downs was paved with white concrete. I could not wait to catch the first view of the sea. When Michael and I were older, we were some-times allowed to stand on the back seats with our heads out of the sunroof.

Once we arrived, there was unpacking to do, but as soon as that was finished and Mum had made us tea, we had our first look at the sea. If it was high tide, we ran to the edge and skimmed stones over the waves. If the tide was out, we had a quick paddle before returning for supper and bed. It had been a long day.

We went to the beach on most days, but it depended on the weather how long we stayed. When the sun shone, the beach, became busy with other families. On windy days there could be a race to find shelter among the breakwaters. It might also depend on whether the tide was in or out as there was much more to do when there was sand to play on. It was also more fun for Michael, and later Robert, to paddle and play in the little waves.

Mummy would always bring diluted orange squash in a large glass bottle, a flask of tea and apples and biscuits. Sometimes we even took a rather hefty portable radio. We often rented a house or flat that was close to the beach and if we decided to stay out all day, Mummy would go back to make sandwiches for lunch.

I liked finding different shops where I could spend my holiday money. In Lancing there was one shop which sold small framed pictures, pens, crayons and cards and postcards. Once when I was going through a stage of wanting a dog, I bought a picture of a red setter and kept it for ages. However, although we had several different pets, we never did have a dog.

There was also a shop that sold peppermint iced lollies. Sometimes all the peppermint flavour had sunk to the bottom of the lolly so if you sucked it upside down it was even more delicious, but they melted very quickly.

They also sold ice cream wafers which were my favourite for a while. A wafer was a small slab of ice cream between two oblong wafer biscuits. As you licked the ice cream round the edges and it started melting, the wafers squashed closer and closer together until there was hardly any ice cream left and you could munch the last bits until all of it was gone.

There was also a big Co-op where, after we had chosen our groceries and paid the lady, she put the money and our bill into a small can like container. She then hooked it on to a wire where it whizzed away to a high window at the end of the shop. After a pause, the container whizzed back with our change and receipt. I found the whole process really interesting.

I also remember a little shop which looked like a green shed. In the window there were glass plates on stands with cakes and buns on white paper doilies. We often bought the small round doughnuts which were warm and sugary with lots of red jam in the middle. This sometimes squelched out into the bag before we ate them on the beach.

Lancing beach was all pebbles until the tide went out. We paddled and swam and made big stone castles and skimmed flat pebbles over the waves. When the tide was out there was plenty of sand and we made sandcastles, dug holes, played games like French Cricket, Pig in the Middle or simply ran in and out of the sea. We also caught shrimps and crabs with shrimping nets. A shrimping net was a wooden pole with a net at the end attached to a semicircular frame which was pushed along the sand in front of you.

It was best to do this where the sea was shallow and the little waves were slowing down on the ribbed sand. Any sea creatures, mainly shrimps and dabs, and maybe a small crab or two, would be scooped over the wooden edge into the net. We put them in a bucket of water for a while so we could look at them, but we always returned them to the sea before going home.

In those days the buckets and spades were made of metal and the spades had wooden handles. The buckets were painted in bright shining colours with pictures of seaside things on the outside. Michael and I had a small and a large one each as the sand was perfect for making sand pies. Daddy was brilliant at making big complicated castles with towers and tunnels and moats which slowly filled up when the tide started coming in. When the whole castle started collapsing, Michael and I would stand on the top singing, 'I'm the king of the castle, get down you dirty rascal,' until the castle was gone. Then we ran up the beach to get away from the waves.

When the tide went out, it also revealed areas of small rocks covered in green seaweed. Among them were pools with all kinds of little sea creatures in them, shrimps, crabs big and small, sometimes hermit crabs, anemones and other colours of seaweed. We had fun trying to catch them in our hands and shrieking if they got away then gently lowering them into the water in our buckets.

Long breakwaters divided the beach areas at Lancing. They stretched from near the top of the beach down on to the sand and further into the sea. When the tide was out, thousands of tiny limpets could be seen amongst the slippery green seaweed clinging to the wood. These tiny limpet shells were very sharp and made painful scratches when we slipped on them. If I went into the sea after being scratched they stung like mad. However, when the tide was in, the breakwaters were great for jumping off, and we spent ages climbing up and throwing ourselves into the water until the tide went out again.

One year Daddy bought some large tyre inner tubes which were terrific for swimming with but we had to be careful the valves did not scratch our backs.

When I was little, my skirts were tucked into my knickers for paddling and I sometimes wore shorts and dungarees. I had at least one knitted costume which most uncomfortably sagged down to my knees, well almost to my knees, when it was wet. It also took ages to dry. Luckily the world of fabrics was moving on and I eventually had a red elasticated 'bubble' nylon costume which not only still fitted when it was wet but dried very quickly.

I loved going for early morning swims on my own with Daddy. Some mornings we were the only people on the beach. At first the water felt freezing, but after I had splashed about and swam, it was all right. When it was sunny and the sea was calm, if I walked in slowly up to my tummy I could clearly see all the way down to the pebbles.

If I had sunburn, Mummy put calamine lotion on me and it felt very cold and made me go goose pimply. One year I had terrible earache, the family theory was that the cold seawater had got into my ears. Mummy went to the chemist and found me some rubber earplugs which I think helped but I could not hear a thing when they were in.

On windy days we flew kites which Daddy made very well and he helped us to make our own. Sometimes a kite refused to fly and wheeled round and round in the air suddenly crashing down to the beach. There then followed a lot of chat about the length of the tail, the shape and weight of the kite and the wind conditions. But when a kite suddenly flew up and up it was so exciting to see it climbing higher and higher as it pulled on the string.

Sometimes it pulled so hard that the string slipped out of our hands. Then the kite dipped down and the string came down too and trailed through the wet sand as the kite pulled it along. We tried to catch it with scrabbling hands and if we were lucky, we managed to grab it again, all wet and sandy.

Daddy also taught us how to thread a message on to the kite string which would slowly make its way right up to the kite flying so high in the sky. When we wound a kite in, it could have five or six messages on it.

Most days we went on the swing boats and a little roundabout which were on the green by Lancing beach. This was the green which had once been concrete blocks with coils of barbed wire along them. The swing boats were the kind in which two people sat at opposite ends and pulled on ropes to make the swing boat go as high as possible. The roundabout was operated by a man in the middle who turned a big handle. The Mermaid café was nearby at the top of the beach where Mummy and Daddy would have a cup of tea and we had ice creams.

Sometimes, when the weather was not so good, our father would drive us along the coast. If we went one way we ended up in Worthing, or, if we went in the other direction, Shoreham, or Hove and Brighton. There was one thing in Worthing I did not like – it was a shop that sold coffee. They had a machine in the window that roasted the beans. I remember being scared of the machine and the coffee smell and I made my parents walk past very quickly. As I grew older my fear disappeared, but I still walked past the window at a high speed.

Worthing had a very good bookshop and when I had some holiday money to spend I went to see what I could buy. One year I bought a book on different swimming strokes. Then, when I was older and more interested in ballet and the theatre, I bought a book called *Balletomane* which had lovely pictures of dancers.

We often went on the pier in Worthing and several times we paid to go on a wonderful paddle steamer that travelled along the coast to Brighton pier. Sometimes we did the reverse and went from Brighton pier to

Worthing. I loved being on the sea and feeling the wind and seeing the waves go underneath the boat and then rush on to the shore. Daddy always took me down to the engine room where there were huge shiny pistons going round and turning the paddle wheels.

The piers also had amusement arcades. These were big halls where music was played very loudly and there were all kinds of penny machines. Some of them were very simple, you just put a penny in the slot and a big puppet sailor in a glass case would shake and laugh for a short while. On another, you put your hand on a metal plate to have your palm read and a little card came out with you fortune written on it.

The complicated ones were more like games, when the moment you put a penny in the slot a little ball would come out near the top and you had to move it down the board without it disappearing into one of several little holes on the way. If you were successful you could have a free go. Some machines had small grab cranes in them and you had a short time to move a crane around and lower it to open and grab a prize which would be something cheap, like a gob stopper or a little toy.

If you were successful the crane dropped your prize down a hole and then it would come clattering down to a ledge at the front of the machine where you could claim it. The cranes with hooks were much more difficult. There were many other different kinds of machines but the only time I won anything special was on Worthing Pier when I was older. I managed to knock all the pieces of a jigsaw flat with a pin ball to make a complete picture. The prize was an alarm clock with a bell on top and it worked for years.

Sometimes, as a treat, we had a pink stick of peppermint rock. All the way down the middle was red lettering saying Brighton Rock or Worthing Rock. I remember once sucking a stick of rock all the way from Brighton to Lancing and ending with the sorest tongue ever.

It was not unusual for us to meet with other families we knew when we were on holiday and there was one particular visit I shall never forget. We went to see some friends of our parents who also had two children who were older than us. They lived on a converted motor torpedo boat which was moored in Shoreham harbour.

Mummy and Daddy were really delighted to meet their old friends again and the four of them did not stop talking. We children were sent away to a cabin at the other end of the boat where Michael and I were subject to what seemed like hours of bullying and spiteful behaviour. I had never before had to deal with such unkindness and remember shouting at them to stop hurting Michael. At last our torture was over and when asked by the grownups if we had enjoyed ourselves, Michael and I smiled politely and said we had had a lovely time thank you. But as soon as I could get close to her, I whispered to Mummy, 'Please can we go home now?' We did not tell on the other children until much later and Michael and I still call them the horrible children to this day. Other Lancing memories are of driving through Shoreham by the harbour where a power station was being built. It seemed to take years and when Michael was little he called the pile drivers 'pish bangs' which I later learnt was a fine example of onomatopoeia.

When the weather was bad, it was great to be able to go to the cinema and fortunately, close to Lancing station there was one called the Luxor. Here, on wet afternoons, I remember seeing a Just William film and also one about Robin Hood.

Hove was also significant in my young life as it was at the King Alfred baths that I learned to swim. Daddy was very keen for us to become good swimmers and I am deeply grateful to him for taking me there when we were on holiday.

There were two pools, the Major and Minor pool, and they had salt water in them. I learned to swim in the Major Pool and once my instructor took me along to where it was almost too deep for me stand. I looked up at him and said, 'It's a bit deep for me here,' and he said, 'Well you'll have to swim then' and I guess I did.

Mummy used to love having a Turkish Bath when we were on holiday and I seemed to remember the Turkish Baths were at the King Alfred as well.

According to my parents, during the Second World War there was a false story from Germany that the King Alfred had been sunk. Certainly, years earlier, it had been requisitioned by the Navy for training purposes. Like all Royal Navy shore establishments it was given the prefix HMS, so it was known as HMS King Alfred, but being a building, it would have been difficult to sink.

In Lancing, I remember visits to Auntie Alice who lived next door to Big Granny and was also rather fat. Auntie Alice lived with Auntie Robbie who was thin and little. They had lots of shiny furniture and glass cases full of china figures. Tiny keys opened the glass doors. Sometimes I had nightmares about little men walking around on the top of the wardrobe where we were staying.

Once when we were visiting, Mummy nearly fainted when Michael was still in the car and it moved forward when it was parked outside Big Granny's bungalow. I saw it move too, but it only went a little way.

I had a friend called Peter who lived in the flats opposite Big Granny and we played together a lot. When the fair came, he was allowed on the Chair o' Planes and I was not. I could hear the music playing *Money is the root of all Evil* until late in the night when it was dark and the lights were orange and yellow. However long we kept going back I never went on the Chair o' Planes, and later they built houses on the green where the fair used to come.

Once, at twilight time, the tide was out and the sun was low, making shadows in the ribbed sand. It was a beautiful evening and I was alone, running and jumping over the pools. I met a girl and she had long hair too. We ran, danced and jumped and laughed together. She was much better at dance jumps than I was and I felt completely happy, but I had to go in as it was late. I never saw her again although I looked the next day and the day after that until we went home.

Later, we went to other seaside places for our holidays, Hayling Island, the Isle of Wight and Lyme Regis are the ones I recall. Once we stayed in a caravan and another time Big Granny came with us when we stayed in a bungalow.

Hayling Island beach was similar to Lancing's but it was interesting to drive over a bridge to the island. I remember hearing people talk about how

58.

'low lying' the island was. That night I lay in bed and was sure I could hear the waves getting nearer and nearer and eventually went to sleep fearful that we were all going to drown in our beds.

From the photographs I have, it seems we had two holidays on the Isle of Wight. I am not sure where the first one was in 1955 but I made friends with some boys and the second in 1956 was in Bembridge. We stayed in a large boarding house and I met children who enjoyed swimming and the beach as much as I did.

The beach was pebbly at the top but halfway down there was a steep drop of about three feet. When the tide was just high enough to cover it we could jump and dive in, it was the most fantastic fun. Unfortunately, I lost my favourite swimming costume on the beach there, and the other thing of note was that there was a tummy bug going round which only my father and I managed to avoid. When we were at the supper table my father tapped the water jug and said in a significant tone of voice, 'It's probably this,' possibly a throwback to his childhood years in Egypt.

My father also enjoyed sailing, but he rarely had the chance to do so. He may have given up after the time he took me out in a small sailing boat and we got stuck on a sandbank and had to be towed off. I was mortified, as all the people in the other boats cheered as we were towed past, but Dad seemed to think it was amusing.

I have very few memories of Lyme Regis, except for the steep hill we had to walk up and down to get to and from the beach.

After that I didn't go holiday with the family because I had joined the Girl Guides and went with them on camps and youth hostelling.

In 1958 I went with Sheila, from down the road and a fellow Guide, on a youth hostelling holiday in the Lake District and my childhood holidays came to an end.

10

Lower 3E
September 1951- September 1952

It was not without excitement and a little apprehension that I returned to school in the September of 1951. I was to be in Lower 3E in a classroom in the main building with Miss Wilmot as our form teacher. The first letter of the teacher's surname was used to identify her form's title, but this year it did not seem to be the case. The mystery was solved when Miss Wilmot signed my autograph book as M. Eardley-Wilmot, hence the apparent anomaly.

I remember liking her a lot; she was fair and firm, so I appreciated the way she taught us. It was not a very large classroom and a bit of a squash for all our desks, but once we were sitting down it was fine.

The desks were much older and had scratch marks on them as well as ink stains. We now kept all our books, rulers and pencil cases in our desks, but took some of them home for homework.

Our morning routine was much the same as in Form 2. The monitor for the week had to check the blackboard was clean and write the day and date in the top right corner. When it was time, Miss Wilmot called out our names from the register and when the bell rang for assembly we all walked along to the Hall. We were now on the second row with the new Form 2 pupils in front of us. I now felt that I really belonged.

It was about this time we were taught calligraphic writing. I found this very difficult because the calligraphic style was designed for right handed people. Despite using a special nib for left handed writers I never really got the hang of it and to this day I write in several different styles.

One of a later teacher's comments at the end of a composition of mine about a desert island, was, 'Attractive to read but untidy to look at,' which was a back-handed compliment if ever there was one.

I made a good friend in Lower 3E - Carole Fisher. Our birthdays were both in December; hers was on Christmas day. Her hair was darker than mine and we both had plaits. We got on very well and sat next to each other in class. Sometimes, she stayed the night at my house and vice versa - usually at weekends.

I loved going to her home. They lived in a village called Shelford which was deep in the countryside. When the kitchen stove was not lit in the summer they had no hot water, and if we wanted to wash our hair her mother would fill up a big pan from the water butt outside and heat it up on an electric ring. Our hair felt soft as silk after washing and rinsing in the rain water.

Once we were to have pigeon for supper. Before cooking it, Carole's mother emptied on to the kitchen table the contents of the plucked pigeon's tummy. It consisted of undigested peas taken from the farmer's field.

Carole and I both cried 'ugheeeer' when we saw the peas but nonetheless we later ate the pigeon. Those days together were very happy. Sometimes I thought I would really like to have a sister, but my brothers were all right really.

Girls like Carole, who lived so far away from school, had to have a 'fog address' where they could go and stay nearer to school if there was a really bad fog. Nottingham had some very thick fogs in those days and the buses in the countryside could get stranded, especially on dark winter evenings. I lived quite a long way from school too, but the roads all had street lights, so although it could be murky I was always able to see my way home.

In Lower 3E we had woodwork classes which I took to straight away. Using a fretsaw, I made a jigsaw of a rabbit. I started off with two identically sized pieces of plywood. On one piece I drew and painted a field with a rabbit in the middle. I then cut the rabbit out in one piece with the fretsaw. I stuck what was left of this piece on to the other, so there was a rabbit shaped cut out in the middle. Then I took the cut out rabbit piece, drew lined shapes on it and very carefully sawed along them to make the jigsaw pieces. The final touch was a coat of light varnish. I was really pleased with it and the whole process gave me a real taste for creating and making.

As our class room was now in the main building, at morning playtime, we first went into the hall for our milk. It was supplied free to all schoolchildren by the Government; a practice that was continued until Margaret Thatcher abolished it when she was Minister of Health.

We'd had milk in the previous year, but a crate was delivered to our class room in the Hut. In the hall, older girls who were milk monitors, served a small bottle of milk and a straw to each pupil.

In the winter the milk was sometimes so cold the bottles froze our hands and it was difficult to drink it quickly because a plug of ice had formed in the neck of the bottle. There was also a big tray of buns for sale. A bun could help the cold milk go down; the best ones had thin icing on them but usually they were plain, or sometime there were doughnuts, but you had to be in the queue as soon as possible on doughnut day as they sold out very quickly.

School lunches were also served in the hall. Rows of long tables and benches were set out and there were two tables by the walls where we queued up with our plates. The dinner ladies served us the first course and afterwards the sixth formers helped them serve the puddings.

Many adults, when looking back on school dinners, usually say how much they disliked them, but ours were good. However, there were two or three things I had difficulty in swallowing, especially butter beans and big chunks of beetroot. The puddings were lovely though.

There was often a sponge pudding which came in big trays and cut into square portions. It could be plain, chocolate, or sometimes with dried fruit. There was custard or chocolate sauce to have on top. Everyday there was the alternative of rice pudding with a little dollop of jam.

When everyone at a table had finished a course, someone called out 'Stack!' and the plates were passed along both sides of the table to make two piles, which were taken away. Some pupils had packed lunches and they sat at the cold lunch table. Because there were more pupils than places, there were two sittings for lunch with the older pupils usually going to the second sitting.

In the lunch break we played a variety of games. We used to 'dip' for who was going to be 'it'. For one dipping rhyme everyone stood in a circle with both fists forward, thumbs at the top. The dipper, counting her own fists as well, went round touching each of the others' two fists with each 'potato' and on each 'more', the relevant fist was 'out'. Whoever had the last fist left was 'it' :

One potato, two potato, three potato, four
Five potato, six potato, seven potato, MORE!

There was another one I never could remember properly, it was something like:

Eeni meeny macaraca
Rare, ri, domenaca
Chiceraca,
Rom, pom, push

Then someone was pushed out of the ring and the last person left was 'it' and we would play a chase game like Tiggy Off Ground, or Statues. In Tiggy Off Ground everyone ran around and to avoid being touched or 'dobbed' had to find somewhere to stand off the ground, such as a wall, chair, or step, where you were safe, otherwise you would be the next person to be on. In the Statues game everyone ran around and once you were dobbed you had to stay still as a statue until everyone was a statue and the first person dobbed became' it'. There was also Tiggy Relievio, which involved an agreed area called the den and one catcher who caught people by touching them. If you were caught you had to stand in the den until one of the other players touched you in order to 'relievio' you. But they might get caught trying to 'relievio' you and would have to stand in the den as well and the den could get very full.

We also played a game called Hot Rice which started off with everyone standing in a circle with legs apart and feet next to your neighbour's. Then someone bounced a tennis ball in the middle and whosoever's legs it rolled between became the chaser with the ball. But they could not run with it, they had to throw it at someone and if they were hit then they became a chaser as well. They could now pass the ball to each other but not run with it. By the end, everyone was a chaser and the remaining player was running around like a rabbit to avoid being hit.

There were all sorts of 'dipping' games to decide who was going to be 'it' or sometimes we just played hand clapping games which became faster and faster with the clapping:

My mother said I never should
Play with the gipsies in the wood
If I did, she would say
'Naughty little girl to disobey'.

We also played Sly Fox or What time is it Mr Wolf? two similar games beginning with a girl standing on one side of the playground with her back turned to everyone else and the other participants creeping up on her. In Sly Fox, the game was to creep up on her but she could turn round at any moment and if she saw anybody moving, they had to go back to the starting point.

With the Mr Wolf game, all the creeping up people would say 'What time is it Mr Wolf?' and Mr Wolf, without looking round, might say 'It's two o'clock' and the creeper uppers could take two paces forward. If one of them was then able to touch Mr Wolf, they exchanged places and the game started again. However Mr Wolf could suddenly turn around and say 'It's my suppertime!' and run and try to catch someone before they were back at the start. If someone was caught they would become Mr Wolf.

There were skipping games, either with one girl with her own skipping rope or a long piece of rope where more than one girl could skip in while two others turned the rope. There was one with the rhyme:

All in together girls, never mind the weather girls,
When it is your birthday, you must run in,
January, February, March, April etc..

People skipped in when their birthday month was sung. If the rope became too crowded it could end in chaos and a terrible rope crash but if all went well, by the time December, my birthday month was sung, they carried on turning the rope and the song was sung again with one alteration:

All in together girls, never mind the weather girls,
When it is your birthday, you must run OUT,

64.

January, February, March, April etc.. .

and each one skipped out in the same way as when they skipped in.

***

It was in February 1952 that the whole school was summoned to a Special Assembly. The dinner ladies were in the hall as well, and I noticed some of them were crying. Miss Milford looked very serious, then she told us that our King, - George VI - had died.

I was quite affected by this announcement, not so much because the king had died, but because the dinner ladies were so upset.

***

My love of books continued. I must have read hundreds but the ones I particularly remember from these years were titles from Pamela Brown's series that began with *The Swish of the Curtain*, including *Maddy Alone* and *Family Playbill*, about a Victorian theatrical family, also by Pamela Brown. There were books about a girl called Matty who wanted to get into films. My enjoyment of theatrical topics is clear. I also read classics like *Treasure Island, Little Women* and *Good Wives*. I was and still am, fascinated by the very old fairy stories by The brothers Grimm and also *The Arabian Nights*. I also enjoyed modern books like *Swallows and Amazons*. I am not sure exactly when I started reading *Biggles* books but I do remember how much I enjoyed them.

By now I had quite a few reference books, such as *The Observer's Book of Wild Flowers, and Birds* and a book on different swimming strokes.

I absolutely loved swimming, but in Nottingham there was no sea to swim in on the way home from school. However there were two indoor swimming pools. One was the Victoria Baths and the other was the Portland Baths which were off Arkwright Street, a little way after Trent Bridge and quite near to home. I do not recall going there very often until I was older and could go on my own, but at weekends in the summer dad would sometimes drive us out to Calverton Lido or Papplewick Lido. That was a real treat.

I remember at Calverton there was a small playground with swings and slides and a metal pole that had four ropes hanging from the top. The idea

65.

was that you and three other newly made friends each grabbed a rope and ran round like mad and the top of the pole revolved faster and faster and you jumped off the ground and held on to the rope as they spread out and lifted you off the ground and you flew. It was a bit like do-it-yourself Chair o'planes, but without the chairs. Sadly, it slowed down far too quickly and then we dashed off to cool down in the pool.

On Sundays, before Dad became more involved in flying at the weekends, he might take Little Granny and Granddad out for a drive and I sometimes went with them. As I mentioned before, Little Granny had quite a nervous disposition and in Clifton Church one Sunday afternoon she looked up at the vaulted roof and said in a doom laden voice, 'Oh Hector, it looks as though it is going to fall on us.'

Suddenly, I wanted to be out of that church right then. And once, when we were having a picnic by the river, some inquisitive cows came near us and she insisted on moving away, saying in her broadest Irish accent, 'I don't like the way they look at you' and she stared hard, eyes wide open, to make the point. However, those Sunday afternoon country outings became less frequent, as Dad spent more time at a local airfield flying club, teaching people to fly.

At home our lives settled into a routine. During the week I was up and dressed by seven thirty, ready to have breakfast, which usually included some kind of cereal. My mother bought a wide variety: cornflakes, puffed wheat, grapenuts, which were crunchy and came in a small box and always porridge in the winter.

Mummy cooked the porridge in a double boiler saucepan to avoid it sticking. Non-stick pans had not yet been invented.

We had toast as well, but had no electric toaster so it was cooked under the waist level grill until years later, when Mummy had a new gas stove with an eye level grill. If I had time I might also have a boiled egg; then I was out of the house to catch the bus.

We had a high tea about 6pm which could be fried eggs, sausages, or cold meat, corned beef or spam with chips. Other times it might be soup, or beans and toast, or in the summer, salad, which I did not like.

It may seem that our father was the dominant character at Upavon but it was certainly my mother that held our home life together. She had the wireless on in the kitchen most of the time listening to music programmes like Housewives Choice, Worker's Playtime and Music while you Work. In the school holidays, if it was a tune we all knew, we would sing to it and even sometimes dance around the kitchen.

Looking back, she always seemed to be an ordinary mother and house-wife, but before she'd married she had led quite a glamorous life working on the West End stage as a dancer in reviews and musicals. In those days she had known many of the great stars, but she'd continued to live with my grandmother.

When she was in touring shows away from home she'd kept less sociable hours than most people and remembered eating at odd times.

She met my father when he was staying at her mother's boarding house in Kew and despite her limited domestic experience, she became a very good cook, especially bearing in mind that most groceries did not come off rationing until 1953.

Mummy was always thrifty when it came to household expenses and could make the Sunday joint last until Tuesday; roasting it for lunch on the first day, then cold with chips for supper on the second day, and on the third day, mincing the leftovers for a Shepherd's pie. The meat was minced in a cast iron mincer, which she clamped to the work surface. The chunks of meat were fed in through the top and as the handle was turned round little snakes of the minced meat came out through some holes and onto a plate. It was her sole kitchen gadget for years.

Mummy's roast lunches were delicious, the joint accompanied by roast and mashed potatoes, Yorkshire pudding and vegetables, probably, when available, two each of either cabbage, Brussels sprouts, carrots, fresh peas, and fresh beans.

For most families, life improved noticeably during the 50's. People could afford items that had, in the post-war years, been considered impossible luxuries.

Once we acquired a refrigerator we could have frozen peas, which were kept in a small freezing compartment at the top of the fridge. Mummy made lovely gravy with Oxo or Bisto cooked in the roasting pan and offered the bloody juice from the joint to anyone who liked it. I did.

She also cooked meat stews with onions, carrots, and sometimes dumplings, all in a delicious gravy. Her Shepherd's pies, often accompanied by baked beans or peas, were wonderful. If there was mashed potato and cabbage left over, it became bubble and squeak the next day. We had a chip pan with a wire drainer which always contained at least three inches of lard. They were the best chips ever. She often cooked rabbit, which was also tasty but very bony. We occasionally had salads of lettuce, tomato and cucumber, but I did not eat salad for years, I just could not stand it.

Mother's baking was exceptional and when she could buy the necessary ingredients she made apple pie, treacle tart, made with syrup poured over fresh breadcrumbs in a pastry base, jam or lemon curd tart, or small tarts, flapjack and cake, Victoria sponges, fruit cake and a Christmas cake.

Also she baked rice puddings and we sometimes had tapioca or semolina into which we stirred jam until the pudding went a dubious grey colour but still tasted delicious.

One of my favourite desserts was junket, when a small amount of a dark pink syrupy liquid was added to a saucepan of milk that was just warm enough to curdle and the mixture was poured into small glass bowls and left to cool. After a few hours it set into a lovely kind of custard, not quite as solid as blancmange, and it slipped down very easily,especially when I had tonsillitis.

My mother always encouraged me to cook and when I could I made scones, tarts and had a go at fudge and toffee. However, I almost came to a sticky (sorry) end when I was trying to cut some treacle toffee with a small pointed knife which slipped and went into my wrist, just missing my artery. It did not bleed much but I sensed how scary it was and I felt a bit ill afterwards. Mother went rather pale. Perhaps it brought back the memory of me cutting myself on father's razor. Anyway, the 'toffee incident' taught me, when using a knife, to always cut away from my body.

11

Life at Home

The one thing my mother never learned to do was drive. Our father tried to teach her several times, while Michael and I were sitting in the back. This was hopeless, as every time Mummy made the car hiccup or stall suddenly, Michael and I slid around and shrieked 'Daddy, please don't let mummy drive, Please! Pleeeease!' There were no seatbelts to hold us still then, but even if there had been I doubt if they would have made any difference to our feelings of abject terror.

Fortunately for my father, tea finally came off rationing in 1952. He loved his 'cuppa' and when he worked at home a kettle was constantly steaming on a back gas hob ready for his next pot of tea.

There were no teabags then, just loose tea leaves. My father also used what he called a dunker to save making a whole pot of tea. A dunker was like a piece of cutlery with a small dessert spoon sized egg shape at one end with holes in it. A little lever on the handle opened the egg shape which could then be filled with tea leaves, it was then closed and placed in a mug or cup and boiling water was poured over it. After a couple of minutes the dunker was removed, although Father liked strong tea and often left it in after the milk was added.

He liked toast as well but before he buttered it he always slid the blade of the knife up through the slice. He said it was to let the air in, but I never understood what he meant by that.

When he was shaving, one of my father's little habits was in a very deep voice, to sing:

Hob shoe hob, hob shoe hob
Here a nail and there a nail
And that's well shod

...and he would go on and on, and on. We thought he might have originally heard it on Listen with Mother. Even when Michael and I went into the bathroom, or knocked on the door, to ask him something, he'd continue to sing his reply, replacing some words of the song with his answer. If we asked if we were going out in the car, he might reply:

Yes we are, yes we are
We will all be going out
In the car.

We would then giggle and go and tell Mummy. Unfortunately it could take him ages to sort out the words by which time we were shrieking 'Just tell us daddy, pleeeease!' and then he might then stop singing and say, 'What was the question?' which used to drive us mad.

Another of his habits was to tease us by calling us from a distance, especially if we were in the garden and we would rush to find him, panting, 'Yes daddy?' He then put on a very serious face and would say, 'Where would you have been if I hadn't called you?' and we would say, 'Oh Daddy!' and he would say 'Caught you!' and laugh because he had caught us out again. He could be really irritating.

I also remember him teasing me on the bus. He and I went on few bus journeys together, but a couple of times, when we managed to get a seat upstairs at the front, he would sit there with his foot twiddling one of the two wing nuts that held in place the wide metal cover for the bus number and destination roller.

I was at the age when I had a deep fear of official authority and I whispered 'Daddy don't do that, please, we'll get into trouble' and he would innocently say, 'Do what?' and put his foot down on the floor and then a second or two later it would slowly creep up to the wing nut again and I'd say, 'That!' and so it went on until he laughed and I was in a really bad mood.

On Saturday mornings Daddy often went to a bakers shop in West Bridgford, our local shopping area - no Supermarkets yet - and returned with cakes like cream horns, vanilla slices and jam puffs, one for each of us after lunch, with a cup of tea of course. I thought they were all pretty horrible until the day he brought back a chocolate éclair for me, which was so delicious all his irritating little habits were forgiven - for a while.

In the early 50's there was very little plastic or polythene packaging. On occasions my mother would phone in her order or, more likely, walk down to the grocer's shop, to order a week's groceries. They were delivered in a large cardboard box and items like sugar and dried fruit came in packages of dark blue sugar paper, folded over at the top. Bacon, sausages and cold meats, butter, margarine and lard were wrapped in greaseproof paper. There were no plastic containers for soft fruit or mushrooms. They came in punnets - small baskets of split flexible wood shavings, about an inch wide and long enough to weave in and out to make the basket shape. Sometimes they had a handle over the top and could make useful Christmas gift bags if the fruit had not squelched into the wood.

Before we had a fridge we had a small polystyrene container which was just large enough to hold one block of ice cream. Mr Whippy, the ice cream man, came round in his van on most Saturdays and Sundays and the moment we heard the chimes we shrieked, 'Mum! Dad! Mr Whippys's here!' and usually we were allowed a block of ice cream which immediately went into the container until after lunch.

This container made the most excruciating squeaking sound when the two ends were slid together to enclose the ice cream. However, when there was no ice cream in it my brothers took great delight in continually opening and closing it until someone cracked, and shouting at them put the container where they could not reach it.

As well as mummy's groceries, milk in glass bottles and bread were delivered, also soft drinks by the Corona man. Each Monday he left a bottle of Orange Squash, Dandelion and Burdock and Ice Cream Soda and some-times Raspberryade.

There was nothing like dropping a lump of ice cream into a glass of cream soda. It bubbled and foamed and was a real experience to drink. The bottles had resealable swing tops which kept in the fizz and they had a deposit on them so we always returned the empties. I remember that mother sometimes brought home Kia-Ora Orange Squash or Rose's Lime Cordial and Ribena which I thought was tasteless if it was diluted too much.

The coal man made regular calls every winter, carrying a huge sack of coal on his back which he tipped into the coal shed. There would be several of these and also coke for the kitchen stove. The coal man was always covered in coal dust and looked as though he had been down the coal mine.

Another person that came round once a year was the French onion seller. He wore a black beret and rode round on a bike which was loaded with strings of onions hanging everywhere, over the back wheel, crossbar and handlebars. I don't think Mummy ever bought any, but I really enjoyed seeing him coming along the road.

Then of course, there was the Rag and Bone man. He came round regularly sitting on his cart which was pulled by a docile horse. He collected old clothes and junk that people did not want, calling out the words, 'Rag and Bone' in an incomprehensible manner which could be reduced to one syllable like 'Rone!' If it was a quiet day I could hear him coming up the road with his call of 'Rone! Rone!" interspersed with the gentle clip clopping of the horse's hooves.

***

About this time I must have started going to ballet classes. I think they were my first dance classes but my memories of them are vague. They took place in a large front room in the teacher's house. The other pupils were all girls and I did not know any of them.

The teacher was very tall and thin with a droopy bun hairstyle and when there was music playing she would be doing the arm movements with us with her eyes closed as though she was in another world. I had a basic knowledge of floor and barre exercises before I went there, but where I had learnt them I do not know.

I doubt if my dancer mother taught these to me, but it is possible that as a game she used to get me to try the foot positions. Anyway, we were all being rehearsed for a dance called Spring's Awakening, where we started off on the floor asleep and as the music played, gradually awoke and danced around.

We all found it quite difficult to time our steps to the music, which was rather dribbly and without a clear tempo. I did not enjoy the dancing very much but we wore a nice costume, which my mother said was rather complicated to make.

Mine was pale lilac and comprised of a bathing costume shape underneath with a short tunic of a soft floaty material on top. There was also a garland of imitation flowers pinned over the costume somewhere and another one as a headdress.

It was winter time and I remember we were all goose pimply cold. I have no recollection of the show at all. Maybe I was frozen numb. So much for Spring's Awakening!

I went to a few other dance classes and once we were learning a dance with tambourines. I had a lovely tambourine of my own bedecked with ribbons, which I treasured. But when I took it to a class on a bus I stood up to go down the stairs and the bus bumped and the tambourine slipped out of my grasp, bounced down the stairs and rolled off the bus on to the road. I was horrified and came down the stairs as quickly as I could.

The conductor had rung the bell three times and the bus had come to a halt well ahead of my stop. He asked me if I wanted to get off the bus to find it. I was torn between my love of the tambourine and being scared of finding myself in a place I was not familiar with, so I refused, but felt very miserable about it. I borrowed one of the class tambourines for the lesson but it was not the same.

I also learnt to tap dance, which I loved. My shoes were bright red with a slightly raised heel and red ribbon tied in a bow over the foot. However, eventually I stopped going to dance classes as my interests were changing more to the acting side of theatre and I took Elocution, now more commonly known as Speech lessons. They were one to one, and I could have them at school, in the lunch hour or at the end of the school day.

My first teacher was called Mrs Hamilton. She had grey hair and wore glasses and seemed rather fierce until I became used to her. I really enjoyed learning poetry and speeches. My love of drama and the theatre was steadily growing.

It must have been about this time that things were moving in the grand-parents' area. I am not exactly sure when my father's parents moved to Nottingham, but with my Big Granny in mind, my parents had an extension built on the ground floor which ran all the way across the back of the house.

There was a lavatory and coalhouse on one side, a covered 'loggia' in the middle, overlooked by the kitchen and a room at the other side also accessed from Daddy's office. This was to be a bedroom for Big Granny. There was also a door so she could cross the loggia to get to the lavatory at night.

Looking back, I see it was a generous gesture of my father to afford all this. However it was not without incident. We needed a new concrete path laid around the back of the house and a long straight one down to the garage. Michael decided to ride his tricycle down the path before the cement was dry and made tyre marks in it. Part of it had to be completely relaid. What a boy!

Birthdays & Christmas

When we were young children we always celebrated birthdays with tea parties, apart from the year when Michael and I had whooping cough. Friends were invited for games and tea, and Mummy always made a cake with icing and candles and we had jelly, blancmange and sandwiches. Sometimes we had sausage rolls and small bridge rolls with mushy chopped boiled egg on them - they were delicious.

Thinking back now, we seldom had potato crisps at parties. When we did there were no different flavours, they were plain and came in small bags with salt in a little twist of blue paper to shake over them. When we were very young we had diluted orange squash to drink but once the Corona man started calling, fizzy drinks crept on to the menu.

Daddy was wonderful on those party occasions, organising Lucky Dips so that each guest could take home a gift. I remember him one year dressing up as Father Christmas with a long white beard and putting on a funny old man voice as each guest came up for a present.

Pretending to be deaf, he would ask the name of each child and then repeat it back to them, completely incorrectly. This could be very funny, but he had to be careful not to drag out his mispronunciation for too long or the young guest would start shouting or crying, desperate to receive a gift.

We played games like Musical Bumps, Musical Chairs, Pass the Parcel, Blind Man's Bluff, Here we go Gathering Nuts in May, Oranges and Lemons, The Mulberry Bush, Hunt the Thimble (colder, cold, getting warmer ...) and The Farmer's in his Den.

Even when we were older we continued to play some of the younger games, but added Postman's Knock, Spinning the Trencher, Hide and Seek, Sardines, Consequences, Charades, and Find the Ring. The most memorable children's party I ever went to was at my friend Elisabeth Weller's home.

Elisabeth lived in a large house in Southwell which was a vicarage as her father was a clergyman. Elisabeth's birthday, like mine, was close to Christmas and her parents held a double party, for her birthday and for Christmas. I was invited, and the house looked lovely inside.

There were garlands, lights, baubles and greenery everywhere I looked. In one room there was a huge Christmas tree with a star on the top and a very long table with a white tablecloth covered in little decorations, crackers, holly, candles and glitter dust; it looked beautiful. At teatime everyone rushed round looking for their place names and once found, sat down and started pulling the crackers. It was very noisy.

We all ended up with a little toy each and paper crowns which kept slipping down over our noses. After tea we played games and sang carols. I did not know many of the other children, but it did not matter as everyone was so friendly.

When I left it was dark and very frosty outside. I turned to wave goodbye to Elisabeth and noticed that the light from the windows made the frosty leaves and paths glitter. I could hear laughter and carol singing still going on inside. It was like a Christmas picture and I felt very happy.

***

I loved Christmas. We had a large box of decorations which was kept in the loft. When Daddy could be persuaded, he brought it down from the loft a few days before Christmas. We could then check what would still be good for this year, and what was squashed and needed replacing.

Usually it was the paper chains that had suffered most, so on the way home from school I would call in at Woolworths, which we called Woolies. There I would buy several packs of paper chain strips. Some years, if I had time, I would cut the strips in to four pieces, one cut lengthwise and one across the middle. They made really tiny chains which were a bit fiddly but looked very pretty. One year, when Robert was a toddler, I used a length of turquoise crepe paper to stick nursery rhyme characters on and we put it up in the dining room as a frieze.

As a family we were very thrifty and enjoyed making things, which was probably a hangover from the war and post war days of shortages. As well as decorations, we made Christmas cards and sometimes presents. Mummy told me that Little Granny and Granddad used to save wrapping paper and string from one Christmas to another. Unfortunately, when Sellotape was invented it was difficult to unwrap presents without tearing the paper.

Some of our bigger presents, like bikes, were second hand but our parents went to a lot of trouble to find us what we would like. When I was older they gave me a fabulous Raleigh drop handlebar racing bike; it had gears and a dynamo and the frame was a gold colour. I loved it.

My parents had rules about Christmas, the first one being that we were not allowed to bring the tree indoors until Christmas Eve, by which time a certain high level of hysteria had been reached. Some years when we were was so fed up with waiting for Daddy to sort the tree and I was strong enough, I used to do it myself, filling a bucket with soil and wedging the tree in it and carrying it indoors.

Sometimes carol singers came round on Christmas Eve. They used to sing under a street light outside our house. We might go out and join them but usually we gave them a few mince pies and some money and then rushed back to our cosy fireside, desperate for bedtime to come so we could hang up our socks at the end of our beds. When Michael and I shared a bedroom for a while, I remember us waking up early on Christmas mornings when it was still dark and asking if the other one was awake.

I often pretended to be asleep if Michael whispered to me as I knew our parents would not be pleased if we disturbed them. However, one early Christmas morning we were both awake and decided to look in our socks to see what Father Christmas had left. We found a variety of musical instruments: whistles, kazoos and Michael had a drum.

We had to try them out. Suddenly the door opened and our father was standing there in his pyjamas, in a great rage, 'What DO you think you are doing? Do you know what time it is?'

Well, we knew the answer to the first question but not the second, so he told us 'It's three o'clock in the morning, put everything away and GO BACK TO SLEEP! NOW!' and he turned and disappeared, closing the door very quietly behind him. We two were very quiet for a few seconds, and tried to put everything back into the socks, which was difficult, then we lay down and started giggling and I guess we went back to sleep.

Despite this trauma, exploring Santa's gifts in daylight on Christmas morning holds some of my happiest childhood memories, right down to the tangerine in the toe of the longest sock. However, my children have rarely received any musical instruments from Santa.

Next rule: on Christmas day, after our breakfast, we had to wait until everyone else was up, including grandparents, if they were staying, who also had to have had breakfast. The lounge always looked lovely with a fire in the grate, Christmas cards everywhere, decorations strung across the room; the tree by the window with its lights on and covered in shiny baubles, tinsel, and garlands. Beneath it, there were the Christmas presents, some of which must have been hidden away for weeks. Close by, we children sat ready to go.

Daddy was the most terrible tease; often he would wait until everyone else was in the lounge then pop his head round the door and say, 'Oh there you are - is everyone ready? - I'll just get myself a cup of tea' and we would say with forced politeness 'Yes! - we're waiting for you! HURRY UP!' With a cup of tea already in his hand he would come straight in and say, 'Well, what are you waiting for?' Another Christmas rule was that any presents that had come through the post could not be opened until after lunch.

The first Christmas present I particularly remember was a wind up gramophone which my parents gave me. It played 78rpm records. There were small needles of which one was fixed into the head which was a little speaker in itself. Once the gramophone was wound up and the turntable was revolving with a record on top, the head was placed carefully on to the record so that the needle gently rested in an outer groove.

To avoid spoiling the record, the needle had to be changed after each one was played but there were some needles that lasted for longer. The needles came in little tins.

I was given some very strange records, some of which must have belonged to my father: *The Indian Love Lyrics*, *It Ain't Gonna Rain No More No More*, and a couple of Danny Kaye records, *Bloop Bleep* was one. But

78.

I slowly built up a collection of my own, including another of Danny Kaye singing *I'm Hans Christian Anderson* and *Thumbelina*, but my taste changed as the years went by. Later on I was given an electric record player which sounded much better and I used to play Elvis Presley down the phone to my friend Kay.

On Christmas morning, after the present opening, if it was a sunny frosty day Daddy would take us children out for a walk with Robert in the pram. Mummy stayed at home to get on with the Christmas lunch and Big Granny would help her, especially when she was living with us. If Little Granny and Granddad were with us we stayed at home to spend time with them.

After Robert was out of his cot, we swapped bedrooms and he moved in with Michael and I had the small bedroom to myself. However, I was always moved out for the Christmases when Little Granny and Granddad came to stay, when I was temporarily moved to a camp bed downstairs. I do remember I was not pleased.

Christmas lunch was usually about 2 o'clock and as it was a special occasion, held in the dining room, where Daddy's office things had been cleared away. If the fire had not been going for long enough, the room could feel cold when we started lunch.

Looking back, Mummy organised it all really well. She cooked a turkey and sometimes also a ham, with all the trimmings, even Yorkshire pudding! The best china came out, it was very pretty with a pink clover design around the plates. There was never much alcohol, maybe a bottle of wine and some beer as it was a special occasion. When I was older I was allowed cider and there was sherry before the meal for the adults. Our lovely Big Granny could get very merry on a sherry, in fact, she was often the heart and soul of the party. She had twinkly eyes which Uncle Bert and my cousins Mercedes and Sarah were lucky to inherit.

I have mentioned before that Mummy was a great at baking. At Chrismas time she cooked lovely mince pies and Christmas puddings. Brandy was poured over the pudding and Mummy entered the dining room with the flaming dish. To accompany it, and the mince pies, we usually had custard made with Bird's Custard powder. It was only later, when we had a fridge, that ice cream was on the menu. But early on I do not recall cream of any kind being on offer.

By the time we had finished eating it was very warm in the dining room and the coals in the fire were glowing red. It was time to clear up and move back into the lounge for a doze and open the remaining presents that had arrived in the post.

When I was old enough, I helped Mummy with some of the food preparation and, of course, laying the table, which was fun at Christmas. I also helped clear away and when Granddad was around he was a huge help with this, if a bit manic. The washing up was left till later and at some time there would be quiet for the Queen's Christmas message on the radio. It wasn't televised until 1957.

While the grandparents were falling asleep in their chairs, we fell on the presents that had come in the post. They were wrapped in brown paper and string and once we had undone that layer, there was another of Christmas paper underneath. My godmother, Mrs Lawton, used to send me a present, as did Auntie Kath, Mummy's friend, and Uncle Bert.

Then everyone amused themselves until teatime. One year I was given a large jigsaw which was unusually made of thick board. It occupied me for hours. The picture was of a family on horseback walking by tall bushes of rhododendrons. It was incredibly difficult to finish, as the flowers were all very similar. I kept that jigsaw for years. Michael played with his Meccano and in later years, Lego. I would often spend the afternoon and evening reading one of the books some kind relation had given to me.

At teatime there were turkey sandwiches and the Christmas cake, baked weeks earlier, when we all had a stir and a wish. It was now iced and looked lovely on the tea trolley with a Christmassy ruffle around it.

Later we children said our goodnights and thank you's for a lovely Christmas and went to bed and slept late. The last rule was that we had to write thank you letters, by the end of Boxing Day.

13

Upper 3F
September 1952 – September 1953

In 1952 I took the 11 plus exam, although I was young to do so. One Saturday morning, later in the year, my father called me into my parents' bedroom where he was still in bed chatting with my brothers.

When I entered he waved a letter in his hand and looking extremely pleased, then he gave me the biggest hug ever. I was baffled by this sudden physical demonstration of affection, but it turned out I had passed the 11 plus and there was a chance I would gain a scholarship to the High School.

However, I was not that lucky. I could have gone to the local Grammar School, but my father decided to pay the fees and keep me on at the High School. It did not mean much to me at the time as I was sheltered from any discussions my parents had about making a choice. Looking back now I am truly grateful to my father for affording me such a good education, but he never hugged me like that again.

So, in September we all went up a year into the Upper 3rds. Some form mates had left and other new girls came in. Suddenly our form was bigger than the previous year. Carole Fisher was still my closest friend, but several of the new girls were also to become lifelong friends. Carol Chell, dark-haired and pretty, from Burleigh Road days was one of them, also Elisabeth Weller, a strong, sporty girl, and Anne Yates, who could be mischievous and always seemed a step ahead of most of us in the boyfriend stakes.

Our form was called U3F, which today sounds like a rock band. Miss Ferris was our form teacher and also taught us French. She was slightly built, with grey hair and quietly spoken. This was the year when we had to decide whether we preferred to learn French or German. Only two or three chose German. I wondered later whether this was some kind of hangover about all things German after the war.

Our class room was in C block - C 3, and we could now use a

different set of lavatories - C or B Vestibule. All the lavatory and hand washing cloakrooms, politely known as 'Vestibules,' were clean but cold in winter. Later on, when we were older, we could use A Vestibule which was in the big A block and was posher and warmer and had machines for sanitary things.

One day, when we were in the gym for a PE class, we were assessed for minor physical defects, such as flat feet, pigeon toes, and general poor posture. Those who were judged to have a problem were instructed to attend remedial classes in the lunch hour.

I was described as having a hollow back (apparently I stuck out my bottom) and I had to do exercises such as clutching my knees to my chest and rocking backwards and forwards along my spine, to try and bend it back. I also had to learn to tuck my bottom in more when standing and walking. Well, at least my feet passed the test so Mummy's raised up new shoes strategy must have worked.

We now had many more text books than before and to preserve their condition we had to cover each one with brown paper. Miss Ferris took us through this procedure once and then we were expected to cover the others when we took them home.

We also had our first science classes in the Chemistry Lab. The experiment I remember most clearly was one about heat conduction. The teacher demonstrated it first. She clamped a metal bar at right angles to an upright one so it was firmly fixed horizontally about 18 inches above the bench surface. She then used some very thick fat to stick a row of dried peas along the top of the horizontal bar.

Then she placed a lit Bunsen burner under one end. As the bar heated up, the fat under the first pea melted and the pea fell off. Then, gradually all the fat was melted as the heat was 'conducted' along the metal bar and one by one each pea fell off. I was very impressed.

It was about this time that Katherine and Alison moved away from Ellesmere Road to live in Cheam, which is south of London, and I never saw them again. I really missed them as we'd enjoyed some wonderful times together, especially sharing books and swapping comics as they used

82.

to get School Friend. We liked dressing up and acting out stories, playing silly games in their chicken coop, climbing trees and swinging down to the ground on slender ash saplings and in winter, sledging in the snow.

A couple of times their parents had invited me to go with them to follow the local hunt. They were not riders, so we followed by car, or on foot, if the hunt disappeared across the fields. Although I had read a bit about hunting, at first I found the reality puzzling, but was soon swept along with the other foot followers in the excitement of the chase in an unfamiliar part of the countryside.

The second time we found ourselves close to the hunters just after the fox had been caught. I found the 'blooding' of the young people weird and upsetting. Who on earth would want their face to be daubed with blood? I can't remember how it was explained to me, but the experience of seeing it undoubtedly affected my view of hunting for ever.

So there were no more morning lifts in Katherine and Alison's family car and I was now going to school on my own. Fortunately, the walk to Valley Road was no longer necessary. The roads had been made up and the 24 bus now came to its new terminus at the top of the hill near our house. There, it turned round and came down the hill to the first bus stop; which I could see from my parents' bedroom. In the winter the mornings could be freezing cold and I used to leave the house as late as possible and then run to the stop. If my timing was right I only had to wait a minute or two before the bus came.

I always sat on the top deck, and if there was room I liked to sit at the front to see the river when we went over Trent Bridge. Those were days when smoking was permitted upstairs and I left the freezing foggy air outside for the cosy cigarette fug of the top deck. There was no air conditioning so the windows were often steamed up and passengers wiped porthole shapes on the windows so they could see outside.

There was a conductor who rang the bell for the driver to stop and start the bus, one ding to stop and two dings to start. The conductor also sold the tickets and he or she had a multi clip board with different coloured tickets for different length journeys and a big leather shoulder bag for the fare money. Each ticket had to be punched so that a small round hole was made in it, which meant it could not be used again. There was a row of numbers at the top and if they added up to 21 that was a lucky ticket.

By now in Nottingham it was not unusual for a bus conductor to be black, but I did not think anything of it. There was no sense of racial prejudice in my upbringing, but there was certainly an awareness of other peoples and cultures. My father had childhood memories of India and Egypt, and my mother had worked with a variety of cultures in the theatre, but I never heard them make a disparaging remark that could be construed as being racial.

On sunny afternoons, when we walked from school down the hill to the town square, I loved to see the way the West Indians chatted and relaxed in the sun on the steps of tall houses on the sunny side of the street.

***

On winter days I have memories of coming home on cold dark afternoons to a cosy front room ('Shut the door!') with a real coal fire burning. This was before a gas fire was put in. Big Granny sat in her armchair on the left hand side of the fireplace and Mummy would bring in the tea trolley with a pot of tea covered with a knitted tea cosy, white bread sandwiches, a slice of shop bought Swiss roll, or a chocolate marsh mallow each, or homemade flapjacks, or jam tarts and sometimes a homemade Victoria sponge with jam in the middle.

We would listen to Children's Hour and then go upstairs to our freezing cold bedrooms to do our homework. Just as the electric fire had warmed up the bedroom, it would be time to turn it off again and go downstairs for supper in the kitchen warmed by the coke stove which had been burning most of the day.

My other clear memory of those cold evenings was at bedtime when Mummy would fill a hot water bottle for me. I remember the rubbery smell as the steaming water was poured in. I also remember the hot coke stove with its glowing coals, the cold orange tiles of the kitchen floor and the windows streaked with condensation. Upstairs, the frost would already be painting the inside of the bedroom windows.

It was about this time, I started wearing a plate, now known as a brace, to even out my teeth. It was made of clear plastic and was shaped to fit in the bottom of my mouth and the front bit curled up and over the top of my lower front teeth. There were some wire bits as well.

Every time I went to the dentist, he tightened something, so it hurt to eat for a couple of days afterwards. Also, food was always being trapped under it, which was embarrassing at school because I had to go to one of the vestibules to take it out and wash it clean.

The dentist was just down the hill from home and he was called Mr Hope, not the best name for a dentist, and he did not say much. Mummy always said how nervous he was, which was no help to me. I became really fed up with having to go there so regularly.

Big Granny had moved in with us by now. She really was very fat and had been put on a diet, which meant she was not supposed to eat any bread. Mummy had to buy her 'Energen' rolls. These were round brown rolls which had the consistency of dried cotton wool. Big Granny always washed up the dishes and found it very difficult not to eat the scrapings of the rice pudding bowl or a slice of bread and jam one of us had left on our plate. Her excuse was always, 'It's a pity to waste it,' which became a family saying.

Big Granny once had an adventurous life. Mummy told us how she and granddad had taken her and her brother away to live in Paris on a boat moored on the Seine. My mother must have been about eleven years old. What an adventure. The boat they lived on was called *Sans Souci*, which can be translated as 'Carefree'. Mummy had shown us photographs of Big Granny at that time. She was young and looked lovely and sort of softly beautiful.

But Granny was quite mischievous. Once when she was returning from France on the ferry, an English customs officer asked her if she had anything to declare and she smiled innocently and took a miniature liqueur out of her handbag and said, 'Only this, officer.'

He waved her through, not knowing that she had a large bottle of the same liqueur in her suitcase.

She was often very jolly but if she had a fit of the giggles she could cry with laughter and tears rolled down her face. This always confused me and I did not know what to say or do. She was called Laura which I thought was a lovely name. I think sometimes she nearly drove Mummy mad, but it was nice to have her to talk to.

Now, she wore a grey net to keep her hair in place and she always had a piece of lint under her thick stocking on her left shin where she had had an ulcer. Most afternoons she sat on the left of the fireplace in the front room where she could watch the world go by.

14.

Seasons & Neighbours

Despite the departure of Katharine and Alison, there were still local friends to play with. Michael, my brother, was growing up too, he must have been about eight, but I don't remember him coming to the fields with us very often. Instead, he made friends with some boys of his own age, down the road by the school.

In the autumn we helped the grown-ups build bonfires and we made guys for November 5th. There was still little traffic on the roads, so we rode our bikes and roller skated without worry. We also played hide and seek and roamed further and further afield, even to the edge of The Spinney. But no further, it was dark and spooky in The Spinney.

When the weather was cold and wet we stayed inside and continued to put on shows, which the adults were obliged to come and watch. Sometimes a friend from school came to stay the night with me and we would have midnight feasts by torchlight after our light had to be off. It was about this time that I went to stay the night with my friend Kay and she introduced me to the delight of cocoa powder and sugar sandwiches.

In the first few weeks after Christmas, I always hoped snow would come. It is difficult for me to express how much I loved snow. In a state of growing excitement I would gaze through the window at gentle falling snowflakes that were disguising my familiar world in a soft blanket.

People's footsteps were muffled and occasional passing cars, with busy windscreen wipers, moved slowly by, their wheels sometimes nudging the almost invisible kerb.

When I could wait no longer, I wrapped up warm and went out. It was so quiet I could hear my wellington boots crunching in the snow. I called on friends and we disturbed the quiet white world with our shouts of happiness. Being near the top of a hill the wind heaped the snow into drifts which were terrific fun to plough through, but it also turned the snowflakes into little freezing daggers which stung our faces. We soon learned to stand with our backs to the wind.

Then, of course, there was the sledging, which was a major delight of my childhood and which I have written about in another chapter. Closer to home it was the fun of snowball fights, the building of snowmen and rolling huge snowballs as big as ourselves. At the end of the day the kitchen airer, which was on a pulley, was draped in wet clothes. Our gloves, caked in half melted snow, were placed at the end over the stove and there were little hissing sounds as the drips fell on the hot surface.

The only annoying thing about snow was that it sometimes fell in the middle of the week and we had to go to school every day. I could get myself into a frantic state of apprehension that it would thaw before the weekend. It sometimes did. If it froze during the thaw the pavements and roads were very icy. We used to love sliding, but sometimes cars skidded all over the road and going to school on the bus became exciting.

Apart from my school work, I continued with my Elocution lessons and Mrs Hamilton entered me for the LAMDA, (London Academy of Music & Dramatic Art) Grade 3, Elocution exam. In March I was thrilled to pass.

The cold months ended and spring came. Now our activities changed from winter pursuits. Wild flowers grew everywhere, in the fields and wasteland, and even in our garden. I learned their names and can still recite them: shepherds purse, rosebay willow herb, red and white campion, ragwort, scarlet pimpernel, coltsfoot, clover, celandines, buttercups, bluebells, bird's eye speedwell, viper's bugloss - and many more!

We threw goosegrass at each other, climbed trees and lay in the fields listening to a skylark high above as we made shapes out of the clouds. We had rhymes about the sun:

Red sky at night – shepherd's delight
Red sky in the morning, shepherds warning!
We learned superstitions such as:
Many red berries on the bushes mean it's going to be a hard winter

And:

Never take May (hawthorn) blossom indoors – it's unlucky

It also smells horrible.

And we learned how to demonstrate the passing of the four seasons with one head of grass:

1) Here's a tree in spring, (*the head of the grass as it is growing*)

2) Here's a tree in summer, (*move the thumb and fingers up the stem stripping off the seed heads, keeping hold of them*)

3) Here's a tree in autumn (*sprinkle the seed heads*)

4) Here's a tree in winter (*the denuded top of the grass*) .

At harvest time, we watched the farmer cutting the crops: wheat, barley or oats. Sometimes the stems were cut with the head of grain still at the top and then tied in bundles to stand in small wigwam shapes called stooks to dry. Then a lorry took them away to be threshed.

However, as technology advanced, the combine harvester arrived and did the whole job like an angry clattering red dragon. It roared across the field in a cloud of dust and chaff, reaping the crop then sorting the grain from the straw. The grain came down a pipe into a container and the straw was turned into neat bales tied up with string which rolled off the back of the huge harvester.

The spiky stubble left in the earth scratched our legs making little cuts which stung in the bath at night, but they had healed up by the next morning. It was a good idea to wear wellington boots so you could not get scratched. Later the earth was turned over by the plough, ready for the sowing of next year's seeds.

There were still vacant plots of wasteland land near us where we collected bugs and caterpillars and put them into jam jars with leaves of the plant on which we had found them. Perforated greaseproof paper was tied over the top of the jar so they could breathe and some we saw turn into chrysalises.

We were not very successful in seeing any of the butterflies hatching because when we took off the paper tops, Mummy insisted we put them out in the loggia which had large windows. Our mother had a fear of birds. It was the fluttering of their wings she could not tolerate, so maybe the thought of butterflies hatching in the house was just too much.

I remember her once or twice coming into the front room, closing the door and saying 'Judy, there's a bird in the loggia - please could you get it out?' and she would not come into the kitchen until the bird had gone. It really was not difficult to free them. I checked the door to Big Granny's room, closed the kitchen door and opened all the loggia windows and the two outside doors. The bird usually escaped quite quickly.

**

More houses were being built around us and all the plots were finally filled. Directly across the road from us a couple moved in, Mr and Mrs Hackford. Harry had a moustache and was quite handsome. He limped badly, as he had been injured in the war, but he enjoyed gardening. We often saw him staring out of the window looking at the smooth earth he had raked for a lawn. Mummy said he looked as though he was willing the grass to grow. His wife, Pamela, looked rather like a film star. She had long wavy red hair and always wore lipstick. They were very friendly and Mummy saw quite a lot of Pamela.

Then a family, the Rains, moved into a new house to the right of the Hackfords. They had chosen to have their kitchen at the front of the house. I thought this was odd, but Mummy said it was a more interesting view from the window over the kitchen sink. There was much more to watch on the road and the school field. I never really got to know their children as they were much younger than me and went to different schools.

On the left side of the Hackfords, a house with a tall pointy gable was built where an elderly mother and her grown-up daughter lived. Next to them, lived an older couple, Mr and Mrs Lancaster (Ashley and Edith) who we children thought were rather posh and snooty. They used to go to Minehead for a holiday every year and always stayed at the same place. They got on quite well with my parents, and it was their house where we watched the coronation on the television.

David and his grandparents lived next to them and on the same side Mrs Mee, Ian's Granny(with the goldfish), then my friend Sheila and her brother Dennis and sister Brenda (the ones that had cake for breakfast) and

90.

Katherine and Alison had lived two doors further down.

On our side of the road I did not know so many people, except Geoffrey Wells and his family. A terrible thing happened to their house. A line of subsidence, caused by coal mining, went under their house. It continued diagonally across the corner of the land we were on and under a house on Haileybury Road.

On one side of the line the land dropped down, about a foot. A dip in Ellesmere road appeared and one side of the Wells' house also dropped. There were cracks in the walls and some of the windows broke. It looked crooked and wonky. Later Geoffrey told my brother that when they lay in bed at night they could hear the house cracking.

The house on Haileybury Road had to be demolished and there was a lot of talk by the adults about 'compensation' and 'rateable value'. However, somehow they managed to prop up and repair the Wells' house so they continued to live there.

Near the Wells lived a rather unusual couple, Mrs Carter and her daughter. Adults always acted oddly when they were mentioned. I thought her daughter was quite glamorous. They both smoked and wore make up and lipstick. I heard that Mrs Carter's husband had gone missing during the war and she 'went off the rails' and had parties in her house for American Servicemen when they were on leave.

We now had some neighbours on the previously empty plot. A couple called Mr and Mrs Jackson Jacks (that really was their name!) had moved in next door. They both had rather red faces and played a lot of golf. They kept themselves to themselves but were friendly enough.

On Haileybury Road more houses had been built opposite the school. At the bottom of our garden another couple moved in and much later my brother told me the man who lived there must have been an insomniac because he used to mow his lawn at three o' clock in the morning.

***

An amazing thing happened in 1953 - sweets came off ration - as well as all the rest of the groceries. I could not believe it at first and asked Mummy if it meant I could buy as many sweets as I liked. She said yes and then I asked her if I could buy the whole shop full. She answered, 'Well, I don't think so - for a start there wouldn't be any left for the other children and secondly you'll need much more pocket money and you'll have to ask Daddy about that! '

Oh, the joys of: jelly babies, sweet cigarettes, liquorice shoe laces, liquorice root, liquorice whirl with an allsort in the middle, sherbet in a tube with a liquorice straw, chewing gum, bubble gum, raspberry drops, pear drops, lemon sherberts, aniseed balls, gobstoppers, dolly mixture, sticks of barley sugar and not forgetting the occasional bag of wine gums Daddy brought back from his factory visits.

***

In June 1953 we watched the coronation on Mr and Mrs Lancaster's television. The screen was very small and the picture in black and white, but we did not know anything better. We children had to be quiet and sit still. In London, crowds of people stood out in the rain for ages waving flags.

I remember the Queen looked very tiny under the huge crown. Everyone was very happy and cheered wildly when she returned to the palace, waving to them from her coach. Because of the rain, all the important guests in the procession had their carriage hoods up and the crowd could not see them. All except for Queen Salote of Tonga, who left her hood down so everyone could see her waving and smiling.

***

I think my father must have sold the Lancasters a domestic water softener because they wanted us all to go for an afternoon visit to taste tea made from the softer water. I was one of the first to be served a cup and I started drinking. It tasted awful, but I didn't dare say anything.

Then an adult had a sip and said, 'There's something wrong with this.'

Daddy tried his and said, 'Too much salt.'

He and Mr Lancaster disappeared into the kitchen to make suitable adjustments to the system. So the tea tasting was a bit of a disaster. I was very relieved I had not drunk more because it made me feel quite ill. The cakes were nice though - but not as good as my mother's.

Years later I heard that the Mr Lancaster had died and Mrs Lancaster sold the house and went to live in Minehead, hoping to meet up with the friends they saw each summer. But some of them had also died and Mummy told me Mrs Lancaster was very lonely there. I thought that was really sad, because although she had a snooty manner she was always very nice to us.

***

It was about this time that a young man came to fly his falcon in the middle of the playing field when the school was closed. It was a thrilling sight and I watched him from my parents' bedroom. He never stayed for very long but I could have watched him for ever.

15

Goose Fair & Sledging

In Nottingham, the big event of every year was the Goose Fair. It took place over a weekend in October. Fairs from all over the country came together, and set up as one giant fairground on several football pitches on an area known as The Forest. Once the fear of catching polio had passed, we went every year. At first it was Mum, Dad, Michael and me, then, when Robert was old enough to sit in a push chair, he came too, but only during the day.

Dad parked the car in a back street near my school, and very excited, we walked up the hill. Dark evenings were the most thrilling. At first we could just make out a glow of light ahead of us and a murmur of sound. As we walked on, the light became brighter, and the sound grew louder, until a cacophony of rumbling machines and music, bells, shouts and screams of excitement filled our ears.

At last, at the top of the hill, suddenly, there it was. The Goose Fair!

It was MASSIVE and spread as far as we could see, a fabulous, noisy panoply of colour and light. As we walked down through the trees we could make out two Big Wheels and tall Helter Skelters towering above the other fairground amusements.

There were hundreds of different stalls selling candy floss, toffee apples, brandy snaps, hot dogs, hot drinks, cold drinks, ice cream and balloons of every shape and size. Once we were down among the stalls the air was filled with smells of frying onions, simmering toffee, whirling drums of candy floss and the oily diesel oil smells from the engines that kept the rides going.

There were stalls for playing hoopla, fishing for numbers, coconut shies, tombolas, or simply choosing a numbered ticket, all to win prizes. The prizes could be anything from a small toy, a goldfish in a plastic bag in water, or a bag of sweets, to the hugest soft toys you could imagine.

There were Carousels, Waltzers and Dodgem cars, as well as gentler roundabouts and swings for little children. When we were small, Mum or Dad came down the Helter Skelter with us, but we were soon able to slide down on our own. The Waltzers could be frighteningly fast. Mum and Dad did not like going on them, so we were not allowed on them until we were much older.

When I was lucky I had a ride on the Big Wheel with Dad. I loved going on the Big Wheel. From the top we could see the whole spread of the fair, lit by hundreds of lights of every colour, chasing and sparkling in the dark air.

Then, of course, we had to have a go at some of the games stalls and every year I nearly won something on the hoopla. Dad bought us toffee apples each or candy floss. I loved watching candy floss being made. Sugary syrup was whirled around in a spinning drum, and magically turned in to a delicious sticky, fluffy pink cotton wool. The stall holder wound it around a long lolly stick and handed it over. Sometimes I chose a toffee apple but candy floss was really my favourite.

When it was time to go home, we left the noise and lights behind to make our way back to the car, clutching balloons. Dad drove us home through the dark streets and we sat in the back licking our fingers still sticky from candy floss.

***

When the snow came and settled, dozens of people made their way through the fields up to the Sledging Hill, pulling or carrying a variety of contraptions ranging from six-seater toboggans to metal trays. Those who arrived early would already be swooping down the hill at what seemed to be tremendous speeds.

At first, I had to rely on rides from friends. Katherine and Alison had terrific sledges and they always shared. Dad made me one, but the sides collapsed inwards on its first downhill ride with him on it. People laughed and I felt excruciatingly sorry for him. I remember being given an old one with a tubular frame and runners with slats of wood for the seat. It was not very good on soft snow as the metal runners cut through to the bumpy ground below, which made the ride very slow.

In the end I made my own out of strong wood with metal brackets to stop the sides collapsing and a kind man at Dad's garage helped fix on the metal runners. I painted 'Punch and Judy' in white on each side and although it was heavy to pull up the hill, it was a really good sledge - one of the best on the hill. There was room for two riders - and it was strong and very fast.

I loved the snow and sledging. In winter time, especially at the weekends, I used to lie in bed trying to keep warm in the early mornings and listen to the wind and wonder if the light creeping round the curtains was bright and white enough to mean snow had fallen.

If it had, there was much sluicking and dashing around, looking for warm socks, gloves, scarves, and bobble hats. Then we rushed out to meet friends and go through the fields to The Sledging Hill. Sometimes parents came as well, but the only time mine came was when Dad tried out his disastrous sledge.

It was so good just to be out there with friends in the cold air and snow. Sometimes there were deep drifts at the side of the fields which we threw ourselves into and had snowball fights. The trudge up the hill pulling the sledge for the next run down was well worth it. Some people sat on their sledges, sometimes three in a row on the really big sledges, but most people preferred to lie on their fronts.

I did, because I seemed to go faster that way. At the top of the hill the idea was to start off bending forward over the sledge, running and pushing it forward, moving faster and faster and at the critical moment throwing yourself forward onto the sledge and you were off - tearing down the hill, holding on tight as it could be bumpy, the air biting into your face and, and at the bottom of the hill, as you slowed down, steering with your feet to either avoid going into the hedge or to go straight through the open gate where it was very bumpy on the other side.

There were crashes when not enough time was given to the sledge in front to get a good start, or when people raced two or more sledges at a time. There was a lot of swerving and intentionally knocking each other off, but it was all very good natured. Sometimes a lone rider would tumble off, because of a bump in the track or they were just going too fast.

When some of the lads from the farms came over with their big sledges, they would overload them with the riders piled up on top of each other. They often tipped over half way down the hill and roared with laughter as they rolled down the rest of the slope. We might have gained a few bruises ourselves but to my knowledge no one was ever badly hurt.

When we rushed home, our sledge runners scraped on the pavements where the snow had melted. In the warm kitchen wellingtons were left by the back door and sopping wet gloves, often with little bits of impacted snow stuck to them, were put somewhere to dry while we skidded round on the tiles in our thick socks. Often, we were very wet, especially if the snow had been thawing, and we had to change all of our clothes.

My most memorable times on The Sledging Hill were when I was older. On one occasion there had been a fall of snow which hung around for several days and was freezing hard as I came home from school in the darkening afternoon. The pavements were very icy and there were deep car tyre marks in the snow and ice on the local roads.

The moment I arrived home I changed into all my snow gear, sometimes wearing socks over gloves still damp from the night before. By then, a couple of friends would have called me to see if I was coming out. Within half an hour we were walking towards the Sledging Hill.

The ice and snow glittered in the street lights as our sledges clunked and bumped behind us scraping over the icy ridges in the roads. Then we struck out along a familiar route through the fields, the standing snow making it light enough to see our way. Here the shadows were deeper along the hedgerows and it was quieter; our footsteps were muffled and the sledges gently hissed over the frosty snow.

At last, over the next stile, loomed The Sledging Hill with a few people already there – we could just hear them talking and see them as small moving figures against the snow covered hillside. We puffed up to the top and said a few hellos before we turned to take our first runs and looked back at the view of Nottingham. From the top of the evening hill the lights of the city spread away into the shadows of the Forest and Mansfield.

It was breathtaking. As far as one could see the city was patterned with

97.

street lights looping and crossing like strands of tiny sequins and it hummed with the sounds of industry and traffic, shunting trucks, hooters and sirens. Beyond rows of tiny white rooftops, some with smoke rising from chimneys, I could see as far as the misty horizon of the Forest near my school.

Closer to us the brighter street lights especially the local orange lights in West Bridgford, were reflected by the hillside where we stood. The full length of the sledge run was clear to see all the way down to the hedge where the gate was open. There, the ruts of the icy surface showed in the light of the two candles in jam jars placed on either side of the bumpy gap which we shot through into the next field at the end of the run.

At about eight o' clock we trudged back across the fields to the orange lit roads closer to home. After gliding silently on the snow our sledges again bumped and grated noisily on the road surface and the hard ice. The hardening frost had made the car tyre tracks brittle beneath our boots. Once home I took off all my sodden outer clothes and stood in front of the kitchen stove in my thick socks to warm my cold hands. Mum had left me supper in the oven and I took it into the front room to eat it in front of the fire and to chat with her and Michael. Then it was time for homework and eventually, bed.

The next day most of the snow had gone.

16

Lower 4M
September 1953 – September 1954

I was eleven and at the end of the summer term the holiday stretched ahead for weeks. I helped with the gardening and laying the table and drying up, of course, but apart from that and keeping my room tidy (sometimes) and so long as I was never late for meals, my time was my own.

Most days I went up to the fields with friends, dodging the yappy Corgi dog at the top of Musters Road, we headed for the gate that led to the first field. We chatted and joked around: climbing fences and trees, searching out wild flowers and exploring new paths.

I kept a nature diary, and once we made a map of the fields, hedgerows and the wood. It was about this time I joined the Girl Guides and so we played tracking games I had learned, which were fun, until we actually lost someone.

Occasionally we played games like Truth, Dare or Promise and if someone got 'Truth' and did not want to answer a question they had to do a forfeit. I do not remember many arguments or tears; we were usually good natured. We also spent hours making bows and arrows, and catapults but never hunted anything that moved.

On wet days, if I stayed at home, I read. My love of books was as strong as ever and I began to enjoy writing my own stories and rhymes. I had a stamp collection, and sometimes swapped stamps with friends. There was a craze for transfers, which I put on everything – including myself. I made models from Airfix kits, usually simple aeroplanes.

Sometimes, on indoor days, friends came round and we dressed up. We no longer put on shows for our parents, but we made up stories for ourselves to perform.

From my parents I had acquired a vast old suitcase that served as a dressing up box. It was full of odds and ends of costumes. Some were saved from fancy dress parades, or parties, or from the dance shows I had been in. There were also some of my mother's old clothes and high heeled shoes, odd lengths of material which could be made into cloaks or long skirts, or with a stretch of the imagination, draped over a chair they could become a throne, or even a mountain.

There is a story about the dressing up suitcase. It was quite big and the lid would not close properly and I kept it under my bed. One hot summer night I woke to hear a little scratching sound. At first I wasn't sure where it came from, then as I listened very hard I realised it was definitely coming from under my bed.

I crawled under and listened and the scratching stopped, so I waited and after several seconds it started again.

At that time the land next to us had not been built on and a crop of ripe barley grew close to our fence. We had had some trouble with mice coming into the kitchen from the field. I suddenly thought that perhaps one field mouse had found its way upstairs and hidden in the dress ups. My raffia skirt would have made a perfect nest.

Now I wasn't sure what to do. I did not want the costumes to get chewed up and there to be mouse droppings in the case. I didn't want to frighten it away in case it found somewhere else to hide, but I had to do something as the scratchy-scratchy sound was keeping me awake.

So I crept into my parents' bedroom. It was quite dark but I could just see my way round to my mother's side of the bed. I gave her a little shake and she was awake immediately.

'Mum,' I whispered, 'I think there's a mouse in the dress ups case'.

'A what? 'she said.

'A mouse. In the dress ups!' I said in my best stage whisper.

'Are you sure?'

'Yes, it's making a little scratching sound and I can't sleep.'

My mother got out of bed and followed me to my bedroom where we put out heads under the bed and listened. There was certainly something in the case.

'We'd better carry it downstairs and leave it to escape in the loggia,' whispered my mum.

So that is why that night Mum and I could be seen creeping down the stairs and out of the back door carrying a rather large case. We kept stopping and listening to see if the mouse was still in there, but there was never a sound. About halfway down the stairs Mum got the giggles and then so did I and we just could not stop. By the time we were able to put the case down in the loggia we were crying with laughter.

We never found the mouse. It either escaped while we were carrying the case or after we left it in the loggia. We never found any droppings and my raffia skirt was intact.

***

My mother often had the sewing machine ready on a table. As well as my dress ups she made me some lovely clothes. First we went to a shop and consulted a pattern book. These huge pattern books were full of pictures of clothes to be made at home. Once we had agreed on a design for a skirt, or blouse, or maybe a dress, we wrote down the pattern number and went to the lady at the counter who took the number and advised what size I would need. Then she went to a drawer and pulled out an envelope with the design, number and size on it. Inside, there was a tissue paper pattern of the shapes that had to be cut out of material before the garment was sewn together.

There was also a list of other items that might be required, like cotton, zips, hooks and eyes etc, and most importantly, how much material to buy. Next we went to look at material. Once I chose a plain pink cotton material for a skirt and for the shirt to wear with it, I chose one that was pink with white vertical stripes. When Mum had finished it I must have looked like a stick of rock!

Our sewing machine was not an electric one; you had to turn a handle to make it work. Soon I was able to use it myself for making simple things. Little did I realise how useful this skill was to be when it came to making costumes for form plays.

Once I made little curtains for a model theatre and clothes for puppets - one of which my brother Michael, for some reason, threw out of an upstairs window. He was so scared of what might happen to him that he bolted the door to the front room where the family were having afternoon tea. I have no idea what happened, as I was out at the time and the puppet was unharmed; even its papier maché head, which had taken me ages to make at school, was still in one piece.

When I think about it, my brother was often mischievous, although the disastrous results of some of his escapades were unintentional. As well as the episode with the jammed gas poker socket and cycling down the new path when the cement was still wet, there was a time he came rushing into the house looking frantic. My mother could hear fire engine sirens.

Michael had been playing with friends on a piece of wasteland down the road and the dried grass had 'caught fire'. He said, 'It wasn't me,' several times. Luckily, the firemen soon extinguished the fire and no permanent damage was done.

And of course there was the year he stuck the plum tree cuttings in the front lawn and they took root. Then, when he was older, he siphoned some petrol from our father's car tank with a bicycle pump and squirted it on to a burning bonfire in the garden.

But, he was a dear brother to me. Yes, of course we used to fight, and we even had wrestling matches on the carpet in the front room and once I broke his watch. He had a gentle nature and was usually very cheerful. He was a skinny little boy with brown eyes and light brown hair. After a haircut he looked decidedly impish and Mum and I called him our 'cheeky boy'. When he went to Miss Marriot's he suddenly looked very grown up in his school uniform. Like me he had only one set of play clothes; and these were very plain, there were none of the bright coloured T shirts and trendy shoes boys have today. When we shared a bedroom, we used to tell each other riddles and I teased him when he said 'rolly', for 'lorry,' and 'maggitch,' for 'magic'.

He was always busy doing something; outdoors he rode his bicycle and dug holes in the garden. When there was a craze for cowboys he dressed up as one and ambushed us around the house with his cap gun. But what he really loved were gadgets and things mechanical. He became bored with Bayko building bricks and moved on to making complicated contraptions

102.

in Meccano. Dad sometimes took him to junk shops where they picked up defunct gadgets which Michael and he took apart. Once, he tried to take his tricycle to pieces.

***

In the school holidays, we often used the Jesse Gray school playground for roller skating and cycling, or we went for longer cycle rides. Sometimes we played cricket or football in one of our gardens or on the road.

There was still little traffic and a very clear view of any approaching car. The only accident I had on the road, which happened before it was made up, was when I was playing cricket with some friends. I threw the ball back to the bowler with such energy I slipped backwards on some gravel and banged the back of my head really badly. There was a huge bump and a little blood and I felt very odd, so Mum made me lie down for a while.

About this time there was a rumour going around that some of the older boys had climbed down on to the railway line under the bridge on Boundary Road. They placed pennies on the line and after a train went over them they were squashed very flat - the pennies that is! To us, that was the height of daring. I saw one of the pennies so it must have been true.

***

One summer we made flying streamers out of a cotton reel, a length of elastic and a narrow strip of crèpe paper, about six feet long.

The elastic was threaded through the centre of the cotton reel; the short end was tied round one of the ends of the paper and gently pulled through so some of the paper was wedged in the cotton reel hole. The other long end of the elastic was tied in a big knot so that it couldn't be pulled out by the streamer. Then you found an open space with no overhead wires, and held on to the long end of the elastic and whirled it round and round and then let go. It would fly high and the streamer trailed out behind it making a graceful arch until it fell to the ground.

If you were with friends and let them all go at the same time, the streamers looked wonderful as they flew up together, but we took care not to stand too close to each other as they could get tangled up in the air.

Looking back I find it amazing how much freedom we had. Our parents

103.

always wanted to know where we were going, and who with, but they were quite happy for us to go wandering off, so long as we came home on time.

My mother had made friends with several neighbours and sometimes managed to have a cup of tea with them. But Robert was still very young and needed a lot of her attention.

At weekends, as a family we went for the occasional picnic, but as far back as I can remember, my father spent at least one day at a local airfield teaching flying. Sometimes I had a birthday party to go to, or I might stay the night with a friend, or one would come and stay with me.

A cinema called The Tudor was just down the hill in West Bridgford. We used to go there, usually for an afternoon showing. Sometimes it was just Mum and me, but I was never allowed to go to the Saturday morning children's pictures.

Mum and Dad did not often go out together in the evenings. But each year there were two special events. One was the Plant Engineers Ball and the other was the Masonic Ladies evening. Each year, Mum had a dress especially made. Although she had very little jewellery, what she had was stylish, and she always looked very glamorous. Dad looked really handsome and rather grand in a white tie and tails.

For these evenings we had a baby sitter. At one point, they employed a young woman who was actually called Elizabeth Taylor, like the film star, I think she was a student as she brought lots of papers with her. She was very nice but a bit stuffy. We were usually in bed when she arrived so we never got the chance to know her very well. Perhaps she was just shy.

17

Shows, Grammar, & Fire Extinguishers

My parents had very different backgrounds, which affected our young lives in both subtle and direct ways. By subtle, I mean in the stories of their past lives. Mum told us how when she was about eleven, the family lived on a boat on the Seine in Paris. She also told us about her older brother Bert, who later on had a motorbike and rode to the North of England where he had his first job.

Mum learned to dance and left school at the age of fourteen. She had many different jobs, such as demonstrating at the Ideal Home Exhibition, or photographic modelling for advertisements before she got into show business.

Mum was quite capable of going into a step routine to music on the radio in the middle of the kitchen. She also believed she must have been one of the first one hundred members of the actors' union, Equity.

She was very young to be travelling at night on her own and told me that early on in her career she was in a show in London that finished late and she had to rush to catch the train to her home in Kew.

It was not a long journey, but being late at night she was wary of whom her travelling companions might be. In those days many of the trains did not have corridors and people sat facing each other in self-contained compartments. Once she was in a compartment there was no way to get out, except when the train stopped at a station.

After a couple of nights, some journalists, who were travelling home at the same time, noticed her and took her under their wing.

'We'll look after you,' they said, 'We're on this train every night,' and for the rest of the shows she felt safe.

She also told us other stories; one about a musical show when she and several other girls were meant to be clock pendulums during a song about a clock. It was a big production number and they were dressed in skirts that were far too long for normal wear, but when they were suspended several feet above the stage by wires, the hems just touched the stage. As the song was sung, the stage hands operated the Kirby wires, so that the girls gently swayed from side to side like clock pendulums. However, one night, something went wrong, and the girls were swung erratically and bumped into one another. This was greeted with hilarity by the audience, and when the girls (who had stopped singing) realised they were not in any danger, they could not stop laughing as the curtain came down.

Mum also said they know if a stage set had been previously used by an American production because on the flats at the side of the stage there were lumps of chewing gum which performers had stuck there before they made an entrance.

She was once in a film with a crowded ballroom scene where couples were dancing. Among them were the two lead characters, who were meant to be having an intimate conversation as they danced. The director complained he could not hear their conversation because dancers' shoes made too much noise. So, they all had to take their shoes off, apart from the leads. As a result several of the girls got splinters in their feet as the studio floor were made of wood.

In another film, for a chorus dance sequence, the costume designer had put the girls in black fishnet stockings. When they started dancing and filming, the director complained the girls' legs looked grey. So they were ordered to remove the stockings and draw a larger mesh fishnet pattern on their legs with black greasepaint. All went well until the girls warmed up under the hot lights and the greasepaint melted and ran down their legs! Mum never told us what happened after that.

In contrast to her stories, in 1919 when my father was nearly eight years old, his father, Fred, who was in the 11th Hussars, was posted to Egypt, and Dad and my grandmother, Little Granny, went with him. Life was very different there and Dad told us how he and some friends would tie the remains of the Sunday joint to some tin cans and put it on the ground away from their parents' eyes. Then they would hide and wait and watch for the vultures to come down to seize the leftover meat and fly away with it, the cans clanking and clattering as they did so.

After Egypt they went on to India and did not return home until 1923. All of this travel did not restrict his education, because wherever they were, he was educated in Roman Catholic schools. Later, on their return to England, he attended the Cavalry School in Aldershot.

My father's knowledge of English poetry was amazing and he would often break into renditions of: The Boy stood on the Burning Deck, The Burial of Sir John Moore after Corunna, as well as The Charge of the Light Brigade, and Hiawatha.

These poems were as familiar to children of his day as are pop songs to the present generation. I can remember most of the words of the first two because I heard him recite them so often. This literary background might suggest why Dad was so strict with us about our use of the English language.

In addition to his dislike of the words 'nice' and 'got' he added two more to his list. If one of us said, 'you know,' in the middle of a sentence he would interrupt with, ' No, I don't know,' which could be very annoying. The other phrase he objected to was: 'ever so' - as in 'it was ever so hot' to which he would say, 'How hot is that?' which was also annoying because everyone knew 'ever so ' meant 'very' or 'really'. He knew that too but he thought we were being lazy with our choice of words.

The other thing that Dad did not like, was me wearing trousers, especially jeans, which I thought was grossly unfair, especially as he did not seem to mind me wearing shorts on the beach, or when I went out in the fields. But when I started going flying with him, which involved clambering in and out of planes he mellowed and said he thought they were a good idea.

However, despite all his dislikes and strictness he took us on lovely summer seaside holidays when he took me swimming in the sea in the early mornings.

***

In September I moved up into Lower 4 M. Mrs Moult was our new class teacher. She was very different to Miss Ferris, younger, louder and bossier, and at times unpredictable. She taught music and needlework and our form classroom was the needlework room on the top floor of B block.

There were no desks, just flat tables so we had to keep our books in lockers, which was a nuisance as there was not much room in them. However as our classroom was often used for needlework classes we did not spend much time there and always had to carry our books around with us.

Science and Biology lessons were always in one of the laboratories; Geography was usually in the geography teacher's room, Art was in one of the art rooms and the other subjects were usually in the same rooms but not our classroom.

I remember History being in a big room in A block, opposite the staff room. Our history teacher, Miss Pretty, was strict and a bit scary and a very good teacher. She was tall, had dark hair and wore glasses. She never wasted a second of a lesson and one of my friends from those schooldays, now living in Canada, reminded me of how Miss Pretty would come out of the staff room and stride across the wide landing to the room where we were waiting for her and say: 'Good morning, sit down, test, number one,' before the door had closed behind her.

We had a very exciting moment in our classroom. Some of the girls were fooling around and one of them managed to knock a fire extinguisher off the wall. The bracket holding it was very wobbly and it crashed straight down to the floor releasing the pressurised contents. A spray of greyish foamy liquid shot out and went everywhere, including the ceiling, the walls and our clothes.

There were shrieks and screams, many of laughter and it was ages before any teacher came to sort it out, by which time most of the spray had subsided. My skirt suffered from a long streak which took some of the colour out. I do not recall us being admonished to any great degree and looking back, I think the powers that be must have known about the wobbly bracket. There was talk and concern about the chemicals in the spray and a couple of the girls did not come in the next day. They were said to be suffering from some kind of shock.

***

108.

About this time, I bullied my mother into letting me have my hair cut. I was fed up with plaits and long hair which was a nuisance when I went swimming. My father had always been firmly against me having short hair, his opinion being, '*A woman's hair is her crowning glory*'.

But my mother gave in and she took me up town to her hairdresser's where I had it cut short. For some reason she insisted I also had a perm and after sitting under the beehive shaped hair dryer, and then having it brushed and combed, I emerged as a curly suburban version of Shirley Temple.

When I returned home with mum I looked in the hall mirror, pulled a face at myself and thought, 'It wasn't meant to be like this'. My dad was furious, so my poor mother pleased nobody. Anyway after a few weeks the perm had flattened considerably and there are some studio photographs of me taken in November 1953 which do not look too bad.

***

Fortunately for me the curriculum at The Nottingham Girls High School put considerable emphasis on drama. Each year there was a school play which was performed by the pupils for a few nights towards the end of the Christmas term. I was hugely excited to be asked to audition for the part of the boy Mamillius, the young son of the main characters, Leontes and Hermione, in Shakespeare's The Winter's Tale.

It was a very small part but I studied the play and learned his lines, one of them being the significant, 'A sad tale's best for winter,' which reflected the plot of the play. However, the part went to Suzanne somebody or other and I was very disappointed. But that December I was taking my Grade 4 LAMDA Elocution exam, so I had plenty to concentrate on and I passed, thanks also to Mrs Hamilton.

Every summer there was a drama competition for which each form put on a short play, or a scene from a longer one. This was the first year we were able to take part. However we were not very successful, as we were not mentioned in the school magazine and I can't even remember what we performed.

That July I passed my Grade 5 LAMDA exam and there would be another drama competition next year.

18.

Girl Guides

In early 1953 I joined the 1st Edwalton Company of the Girl Guides. It was linked to the little country church I went to in Edwalton, about half an hour's walk from home. I was nervous at first, but Sheila Knight, who lived on my road went there too and there was such a friendly atmosphere that I soon felt very much at home.

One evening a week, on Friday, I put on my uniform: blue shirt, navy skirt, Girl Guide belt, red scarf and navy beret. Then Sheila and I went to the church hall; a modern, brick-built establishment, where I learnt the Guide Promise and Law. I soon earned my Guide badge, which was a trefoil and pinned on the scarf.

The Promise we made was:
I promise that I will do my best:
To do my duty to God and the Queen
To help other people at all times;
And to obey the Guide Law.
The Law was:
A Guide's honour is to be trusted.
A Guide is loyal.
A Guide's duty is to be useful and to help others.
A Guide is a friend to all and a sister to every other Guide.
A Guide is courteous.
A Guide is a friend to animals.
A Guide obeys orders.
A Guide smiles and sings under all difficulties.
A Guide is thrifty.
A Guide is pure in thought, in word and in deed.
We learned that a Guide should be prepared in various practical ways, for example: a guide should always carry enough pennies for a phone call

110.

from a public phone box; a clean handkerchief for a First Aid emergency, should it be needed for use as a sterile dressing; and a pencil and paper. Safety pins could come in useful as well and a whistle was a good idea when hiking and camping.

We were kept busy during those evenings, learning how to tie different knots, basic First Aid and preparing for tests for various badges. I passed the Cook's badge; the Homemaker, which included ironing and making beds with hospital corners, which Mum had already taught me as she had taken a Red Cross course before the war. I also passed Toymaker, Artist, Gymnast and Hostess and I still have my shirt with the badges sewn on to prove it!

But it was not all hard work, we played games and had competitions between the different patrols. A Guide company was divided into smaller groups called Patrols. Ours were the names of wild flowers and I was in the White Heather Patrol and later I became the patrol leader.

Each patrol had a small area of its own in the hall where we could sit and plan different projects. For example we used to contribute to the church Summer Fete each year by making things to be sold. One year I decorated small boxes and containers with seaside shells, using the ever useful Airfix glue and put a few bath cubes or a bar of scented soap inside. Then I covered the contents with a layer of shiny cellophane, and the shell covered lid went on top. They looked good and sold well.

Another year we were asked to present a demonstration of country dancing and I was the caller. The dance was 'Gathering Peascods'. Luckily, I had a microphone and could be clearly heard above the music. It was great fun.

Because the 1st Edwalton Guides were out of town we were not part of the larger district known as West Bridgford. However, we did take part in their annual parades, where we marched with the Boy Scouts and other organisations. It was exciting to hear the bands playing. But when it came to other events, like sports or camping competition days, or a swimming gala, we were only able to take part in the inter district events.

I was entered for a rope throwing competition in a camping event but I didn't win anything. However, at the Swimming Gala in the inter district freestyle swimming race which was the final race of the evening, I won! Afterwards, I could hear people saying, 'who's the girl in the red bathing costume?' and it was me!

After taking a glucose tablet just before and doing the best racing dive I could muster, I simply thrashed to the other end and was breathless and shaking when I stopped. They did not need to know that one length of crawl was just about all I could manage.

Edwalton village was in the countryside with farms close by, so many of our activities were connected with the natural world. I learned even more names of wild plants, flowers, grasses and birds. Once, when we were all on a walk, I actually saw a weasel.

In the autumn we had stargazing evenings. I learned to recognise the Milky Way, and the constellations of the Plough, Orion, The Square of Pegasus, Cassiopeia, The Pleiades, and how to find the North Star. I am still mesmerised by a clear night sky, making out the shapes I learned so long ago.

We were taught how to use natural objects like stones, or twigs, or long grasses, to leave a trail, and we tested them by tracking each other. One of my clearest memories of that time was in the field on the corner of the lane that led down to Edwalton village. We were sitting in a sea of deep grass and buttercups with the sun shining above in a blue sky. It was absolutely beautiful.

Although I enjoyed the evenings in the church hall and the badges I could earn, for me, the highlight of being a Guide was the camping. We went to a small permanent campsite just outside Nottingham, called Windmill Hill. At the top of the hill there was an open area surrounded by trees where we pitched our tents. There we learned woodcraft and how to look after ourselves in the open air.

Although there were a few old-fashioned ridge tents that slept two or three, the first time I went camping I slept in a large bell tent with several other guides. We lay on ground sheets in flock padded sleeping bags, if we had them, but I struggled and froze through several camps in a couple of blankets and a thin sheet sleeping bag. It really was difficult to keep warm all night, but I must have convinced myself I had to be tough. Eventually I also acquired a padded sleeping bag and the difference was so amazing I could hardly believe how cosy it could be in a tent at night.

We were taught to brail the tents (roll up the lower walls) to allow fresh air to enter. Our bell tent looked as though it was suspended in the air like a roundabout in a child's playground .

We also learned how to make stands out of stout twigs lashed together with string to support the woodpile, our washing bowls, and to keep our possessions off the ground.

The 'Lats' (for Latrines) were very basic and located in the woods, a short distance from the campsite. Before we arrived a trench had been dug in the ground and hessian walls provided privacy and cubicles. If one was on 'lats' duty, lime had to be spread in the trench each day. After we broke camp the trench was refilled.

All meals were cooked on the camp fire. Hearty breakfasts consisted of porridge which had cooked slowly overnight in a haybox. There was also bacon and sausages sizzling in a huge frying pan. Otherwise it could be scrambled eggs and toast. I still think there is something wonderful about eating breakfast in the open air.

Sometimes we made dampers. These were lengths of dough made from flour with milk or water and twisted around a stick, which was held over the fire to cook. They could taste very smoky.

Days at camp had a structure. The Union Jack was raised every morning while we all stood to attention and the campsite had to look neat and tidy for morning inspection. This inspection was usually carried out by our Captain or another senior Guider and there were marks to be gained for each tent. There would an open discussion, after breakfast, to allocate the duties for the day and comments on the results of the inspection and the marks awarded. There was a rota of camp duties and there were organised games as well as instructive sessions on living outdoors.

We learned how to make a campfire and how the best way to start it was by using a small amount of silver birch bark known as 'punk' placed in the middle of some small dry twigs known as kindling. The punk was lit with a match and as it got going, the kindling caught fire and larger twigs were gradually added. After learning how effective punk was I always carried a small tin of it when I was hiking.

I was never bored. I loved whittling twigs and carving and I acquired a sheath knife, which I certainly would not be allowed to carry today. I even made a fur cover for its leather sheath.

One of my favourite times was the end of the day when supper was over, the washing up had been done and we sat around the campfire wrapped in rugs and singing. As dusk came the logs glowed, the stars came out and we sang: *Camp Fire's Burning, Ging Gang Goolie, Donkey Riding, Found a Peanut, There's a Hole in my Bucket, You'll never get to Heaven, In the Quartermasters Stores*, and many more. At the end of the evening we sang Taps as the flag was lowered:

> *Day is done, Gone the sun*
> *From the hills, from the sea from the sky*
> *All is well, safely rest,*
> *God is nigh.*

Then we said goodnight to each other and retired to our tents.

Sometimes with Guide friends, I went to the local woods where we made a camp fire and cooked experimental camp fire food. I was very proud of a special set of billy cans I'd bought from a camping store. They were two kidney shaped cans, one inside the other and they took up less room than round ones as by placing the two flat sides together you could cook two different items on a small fire.

One of the most disgusting things I ever concocted was a preparation I found in a book. It was an egg I broke into a bowl shaped from half an orange peel and placed on the hot embers. It cooked all right, but orange flavoured egg? Ugh! If we'd lined the orange peel with kitchen foil it might have tasted better.

My friend Sheila remembers how once, when we had cooked a snack on a fire, we were chased off a field by a shouting farmer. We never worked out why, but he was very cross, so we ran away very quickly. Luckily we

114.

had already dampened down the fire.

When we were older some of us guides went on Youth Hostelling weekends, which we loved. We walked long distances and slept in hostel dormitories. It was on one of these trips that I was first introduced to the Peak District in Derbyshire. The combination of the peaks, the soft hills and the rivers in the valleys were a new and unique experience for me. Since then I have returned many times and loved it more with each visit.

***

My First Aid training came in useful, especially when a neighbour carried Robert, screaming his head off, through the back door. He was covered in blood from falling off his tricycle. Mum and Big Granny were horrified at the sight of him. I took over and told Mum to comfort him and Big Granny to make some tea, while I washed off the blood with a clean tea towel and cold water.

It turned out he had no other injuries than a bump on his nose, and his tricycle was undamaged. We had a cup of tea and everyone seemed fine, but I felt shaky the next day.

There was another advantage to being a Guide. Sheila and I had been going to confirmation classes in the vicarage. Being Girl Guides we could wear our Guide uniforms for the ceremony, not the awful white dresses that all the other girls were expected to wear. I was very relieved.

I remember a competition to win a tent in the Girl comic. You had to write in praise of Umbro tents and the one judged best, won. I wrote some alternative words to the song: *'We're a couple of swells'*.

> *We're in the First Edwalton Guides*
> *And we wear bright red ties*
> *We'd like a tent to go to camp*
> *But we haven't got the price,*
> (I can't remember the rest but it ended with)
> *And we'd all like to camp in an Umbro tent!*

Well we did not win a tent but we did win a knife, fork and spoon set in a clip for camping or hiking. We also got a mention in the Girl comic.

I loved my time in the Girl Guides. Hiking, camping and especially songs around the campfire introduced me to sense of camaraderie I have rarely felt since. The practical skills I acquired have stood me in good stead over the years. And when I am away from the ambient light of the city, the night sky is still a constant source of wonder.

19

Theatre & Cinema

I was fast becoming a 'theatrephile,' if there is such a word. I loved dance and drama, and I took every opportunity to see a show - or take part in one. Performance and the theatre were obviously in my blood; my showgirl mother's father was a fine pianist and once had his own orchestra of sixty players known as the 'Sunbeam Orchestra'.

I have already mentioned that my mother had been a dancer. After a mainly classical training influenced by the teachings of of Ninette de Valois and Marie Rambert she had decided on a dancing career. Her first engagement, at the age of fifteen, was in the chorus of a pantomime at the Theatre Royal Glasgow. She kept a scrapbook of the photos and reviews which were extremely enthusiastic about the whole production.

Following that she auditioned successfully for the chorus in several reviews produced at the London Vaudeville theatre by Andre Charlot. She continued in *Charlot's Cabaret Reviews* at the Grosvenor House on Park Lane, and in 1930 was in his production of *Charlot's Masquerade* at the Cambridge theatre, which starred Beatrice Lillie and Anton Dolin.

Mum told us stories about being on tour and having to get used to working in different theatres and living in many different boarding houses. She said that the most important thing dancers required in accommodation was plenty of hot water to bath in. They could get very hot and sweaty on stage and often had body paint to wash off.

Most landladies were used to theatre people, but according to Mum, when some girls came back late they found their landlady had locked them out. They persuaded her to open the door and it was explained that they were working at the theatre and would be late every night.

At another 'digs' as they called them, the landlady had some soup ready for them when they returned. She brought it to the table in a large tureen, took the lid off, and leaned forward to ladle it out, and her wig fell into the soup.

I still have my mother's stage make up box. It is made of cardboard covered in gold paper. The lid fits snugly over the base and on it there is a faded picture of an ornamental garden.

I often used it for my stage make up when I was in shows. It still contains some ancient tubes of Leichner greasepaint and my mother's lucky hare's foot, which she used to brush off surplus rouge and face powder. If only that box could talk, I would love to hear the stories it could tell.

***

We were lucky to have three theatres in Nottingham; the smallest was the Playhouse which housed a repertory company; The Empire, which was much larger, presented lighter Variety entertainment and the Theatre Royal showed touring productions of drama, comedy and at least one week of ballet each year. As soon as I was old enough, my mother took me to see the ballet every year. She always booked us seats in the circle because she liked to be able to see the dancers' feet .

I was always excited before I went to see a show at the Theatre Royal. The seats were all velvety and the massive front of stage curtains were a deep red colour. When we were in our seats other people in the audience would be chatting while I studied the programme. Then the house lights were dimmed, people stopped talking and often someone said, 'Shh! Shh!' as late arrivals hurried to their seats.

The conductor tapped his music stand and the orchestra started to play the overture. If I looked down into the orchestra pit I could see the little lights over the musicians' sheet music. Then silently, the massive curtain went up and the stage lights shone on a magic land and the show began.

I never failed to be enthralled. There was so much to be thrilled by; the dancers, who were so beautiful and skilled, the painted backcloths, the lights. I loved the orchestra setting the mood for gentle moments, for happy times and for danger or excitement. There were times when the percussion and wind instruments could make the whole auditorium shake.

Over several years, *Swan Lake, Coppelia, Giselle, Pineapple Poll,* and *Les Sylphides,* floated in front of my young eyes for the first time, and I was hooked. Even now I cannot hear the closing music of Swan Lake without tears in my eyes.

There was a show which was made up of three short ballets. The one that I particularly remember was a modern ballet called *Carte Blanche* which had a circus setting - the dancers reproduced various acts with mime and dance. It was an irreverent approach to the classical style of ballet, but the image of a young man with a parasol walking across the stage on an imaginary line, as though it was a high tightrope was one of the most convincing mimes I have ever seen. The audience gasped when they thought he was going to fall off and then they laughed. I remember thinking that the dancers were being rather naughty by performing that sort of ballet but mum giggled too.

Mum took me to see other shows as well as ballet. I remember *Desert Song, Perchance to Dream, Salad Days* and *The Boyfriend*. She was particularly excited about seeing Mary Martin in *South Pacific*, who actually washed her hair on stage and sang at the same time – *I'm gonna wash that man right outa my hair*.

As a family, we went to pantomimes: *Jack and the Beanstalk, Robinson Crusoe, Dick Whittington* and *Sinbad the Sailor*. During one of these performances I had my first experience of 3D. When we went into the theatre we were given strange cardboard spectacles with one green lens and the other red.

The first act finished with a shipwreck and towards the end of the interval we were asked to put our 3D specs on. We did so and an underwater scene was projected on to the curtains. It was as though fish came out of the curtains and swam around the auditorium. The effect both startled and amazed us.

We also saw a production of *Little Red Riding Hood* in which the lead was played by a very young Julie Andrews, a budding star at the time. I remember hearing some grown-ups talking about her and saying she would ruin her voice if she kept 'using it like that.'

'Like what?' I thought, but I did not ask.

I have suddenly remembered a production of *Peter Pan* in which I saw

119.

Joan Greenwood play the part of Peter. She had a lovely husky voice and the flying scenes were astonishing. It was a truly magical show.

My mother undoubtedly fed my appetite for the theatre. It was especially lovely for me as our theatre trips were some of the few times I had Mum to myself.

***

Before I was born, my parents kept up with the news by going to news theatres. The shows were about an hour long and when I was still quite young they took me with them. The rolling programmes were made up of several short films, often a cartoon, sometimes a Laurel & Hardy feature, and of course, a newsreel of the current news. The Pathé news always began with crowing cockerel.

The Tudor Cinema in West Bridgford showed 'Big' feature films and shorter black and white films. I vividly recall a series of 'shorts' presented by Edgar Lustgarten, of true life detective stories. There were also Look at Life documentaries, a newsreel and trailers for coming attractions. These programmes were shown continuously, which meant you could go in whenever you liked, even halfway through a film, and also leave when you liked. So you could probably see everything twice if you wanted to!

My mother enjoyed feature films as well as the theatre. She was really keen to see a film called *Dangerous when Wet*, starring Esther Williams and she took me with her. It was about a woman who plans to swim the English Channel. One misty morning when she is practising she gets lost and is rescued by a Frenchman, played by Fernando Lamas.

I thought he was very, very handsome, and so Fernando Lamas became my first heart throb. My mother was not as transfixed by him as I was, she was more interested in Esther Williams and how she coped with the underwater ballet sequence in an animation with Tom and Jerry.

My mother also took me to see *The Red Shoes* starring Moira Shearer, a famous ballet dancer. I enjoyed most of it, but thought the ending was horrible. When we came out Mum asked me what I thought of it and I said I thought it was a bit too bloody. She agreed with me and then said she did not think Moira Shearer was very good in the part because, although her

120.

ballet technique was excellent, she lacked - and I can't remember the word Mum used - perhaps it was 'warmth' or 'soul', but I understood what she meant.

My father rarely went to the cinema with us, but once he took me to see a war film called *Flying Leathernecks*. The film was about the bravery and daring exploits of The Wild Cats Squadron of the US Marine Corps during World War II. I thought it was very exciting. When Major Kirby, played by John Wayne, led his men into the battle over Guadalcanal, he said to them something like, 'I'm going in at tree top level and I want everyone below me.' Dad laughed out loud, he was really enjoying himself.

Once, when I was recovering from flu' and almost better, my mother came into my bedroom and asked me how I was feeling. I told her I felt much better.

'Do you feel well enough to go to the cinema this afternoon?' she asked.

'Oh. Yes!' I said. Later we were heading for The Odeon Cinema in Nottingham, to see the afternoon showing of *Gone with the Wind,* which had an Intermission, something I had never experienced before in the cinema.

We had ice creams. It was the only time I ever knew my mother to play truant. Big Granny was at home so the boys were all right. The film really was an epic, I was gripped by it and so was Mum. Originally it was released in England in 1940, so it is possible my mother missed it first time around. I thought Clark Gable was very handsome.

Eventually I started going to see films with friends and my loyalty to Fernando Lamas swiftly switched to Stewart Granger. He starred in *Scaramouche* and the *Prisoner of Zenda* and several other swashbuckling films in which he often seemed to be duelling with Mel Ferrer.

Then there was *The Purple Mask* with Tony Curtis, *The Crimson Pirate* with Burt Lancaster not forgetting clever, funny Danny Kaye in *The Secret life of Walter Mitty*, and *Hans Christian Anderson*, (I had a 78rpm record of the songs *Inch Worm* and *I'm Hans Christian Anderson*). *Knock on Wood* was hilarious and so of course was *The Court Jester*, with the tongue twister:

121.

'The pellet with the poison is in the vessel with the pestle,
The Chalice from the palace has the brew that is true'
which, Danny's character had to remember to save the day. You try it.

20

Upper 4D
September 1954 – September 1955

My new class teacher was Miss Dodwell. She was gentle, dark-haired, of indeterminate age, and also taught us English. She was a good teacher and the syllabus included Jane Austen novels, which she clearly enjoyed. She often sat at her desk giggling or sighing at the section we were studying.

For my part, I did just not 'get' Jane Austen. I thought all the conventions and manners of the day were daft and the heroes and heroines totally wet.

The other English teacher was Miss Gornall, who was the power house behind drama in the school. Every year she organised the Drama competition and produced the school play. I thought she was wonderful. Although I did not fully appreciate it at the time, Miss Gornall played a significant part in helping me fulfil the aspirations of my schooldays, beginning with casting me in the school play that year.

The play was an alternative version of Rumpelstiltskin, called *The Silver Curlew* by Eleanor Farjeon. My friend, Carol Chell, from Burleigh Road days played the lead, and I played Abe – one of several yokels. There was a song in it about dumplings – I can still remember some of the words:
> ……*Dumplings is good,*
> *Dumplings is glorious, glorious food!*
And a good time was had by all.

***

I have memories of all of our teachers who varied as much in teaching styles as in the way they looked and dressed. Miss Kirkland took us for Geography and was strict and very precise about everything in rather a severe manner. She was always smartly dressed with a short hairstyle and the only time I ever saw her laugh was when we were studying Arabia.

She told us that two large oil pipes crossed over each other in the middle of the country. One of our class, who liked to ask clever questions, (well she was clever) put up her hand and asked, 'Which one crosses over on top?'

Miss Kirkland stared at her for a few seconds and then said, 'You silly cuckoo!' then she burst into laughter and continued, ' How do you expect me to know that?' by which time we were all giggling our heads off.

Our elderly Scripture teacher Miss Wootton, had retired and been replaced by Miss Teather and they were as alike as chalk and cheese. Miss Wootton was an elderly, sweet and gentle character who looked as if she might have time travelled from the old testament. Miss Teather, however, arrived with a loud missionary zeal which was a real shock to start off with.

Miss Pearce taught Biology and was quite young. She later became engaged to be married and one of us went over to speak to her while we were doing class work. When the girl returned to her place she was grinning away.

In our break she said, 'Do you know what Miss Pearce was reading in class?'

'No,' we all answered

'A book called 'Recipes to tempt your man.'

'Aaah, how sweet; she's so lucky etc.. etc...' was the response. Miss Pearce must have wondered why we always smiled knowingly at her when we passed in the corridor.

There was a special large room with a kitchen for our Cookery lessons. We were taught by Miss Jackson and she was an excellent teacher. Although I had learned a great deal about cooking from my mother, I learned even more about the detail in the Cookery classes. Miss Jackson dressed in a snowy white overall, she had dark curly hair and very red cheeks, so she looked a bit like a doll. Her voice was high-pitched and slightly plaintive. She was **very** precise about everything: weighing the exact amounts of ingredients, which utensils to use, how ingredients should be mixed, stirred, rubbed in, creamed, or blended. Not to mention being very careful with the hobs and ovens ALL the time.

We each had to have a white apron, which we had made in needlework, with our name embroidered in large red letters on the bib at the top. I really enjoyed the lessons, apart from the time we had to make a stew and transport it home in a large jar. It was an Irish stew and I had never seen a pale stew before. Somehow I managed to slop a little of it into my bag on the way home. I thought it looked like sick and I could not face eating it. But my parents heated it up and said it was delicious. It had taken me a whole morning to make and they polished it off in five minutes.

As far as Needlework was concerned, I had made quite a few things at home before we had any lessons. But I got off to a bad start when the task was to make a blouse. I had bought what I thought was some lovely pale yellow shiny material, but I was told off because I had not heard the teacher, Mrs Moult, say we should not use shiny material because it slid all over the table and was less easy to handle. She was right, but I managed to complete the blouse - and I enjoyed wearing it.

Later, we learned some simple embroidery and I made mealtime place mats for the family with their names embroidered on them. Also, one year we learned how to work with raffia and cane which I really liked and I made a couple of waste paper baskets and a half finished coolie type hat in green and natural raffia. The mats still survive, but not the baskets or the hat.

Miss Parkinson was our maths teacher, dynamic and bright; she kept us on our toes, but for a while we had a new teacher, Miss Orton, who was short and plump and who was hopeless at discipline. So we played her up. In a lesson, in one of the art rooms, I was sitting with some friends at the back of the class where we set up a skiffle group with our geometry instruments.

Later, Miss Parkinson came into our class room and fiercely admonished the whole class, starting with, 'You ALL know what I'm talking about.'
She then talked about rude, unkind and childish behaviour.
'You came to this school to learn, not play around - I thought better of you.' She continued in the same vein, finishing with a fierce, 'And I do NOT want hear about ANY trouble in future. Do you UNDERSTAND?'
The skiffle group disbanded.
Miss Ferris continued to teach us French and Miss Redditch taught us Latin. I always enjoyed the French lessons and liked Latin, but our Latin

teacher, who must have been a very clever woman, had slightly weird mannerisms. She used to make us giggle because she looked as though she was in a fencing duel when she wrote on the black board. She also, more than once, said the classic line: 'Now girls, look at the board while I run through it.'

Over the years we had several games teachers but I clearly remember Miss Glossop, who was young, thin and very fit and had played hockey for England. We made two day trips to Wembley to watch England play. It was fun to travel on the train with friends and eat a picnic on board before we arrived at our destination. In my picnic box Mum always included a small tin of mandarin oranges, which tasted deliciously refreshing after sandwiches.

Mrs Elphick, was the other games teacher I remember. She was an older woman and wore her hair in two coiled buns over her ears which looked like earphones. Mrs Elphick had a posh voice and in the middle of refereeing a hockey game would call, 'I say, I say, wasn't that a foul?' and everyone just kept on playing. We were used to a referee yelling, 'FOUL!' and play stopped and a free hit or corner was taken.

We also had a gym lesson each week. I was never particularly good at it, but I could climb to the top of the rope and leap over a box with some agility. I think the dancing lessons must have helped.

One of my favourite subjects was Art. There was one large art room on the first floor, between A & B block and a smaller one in B block. I loved the lessons. Miss Stanway was our first Art teacher. She was a diminutive person and a 'quiet' teacher, but even in a large studio, although she spoke softly, we heard every word she said.

On the few times she had to raise her voice it became very strained and slightly comic, but we did not laugh. One summer, word went around that Miss Stanway had a picture in the Summer Exhibition at the Royal Academy and we respected her even more.

Miss Stanway always encouraged me and as I now realise, was very skilled at making suggestions on how to improve a piece of work. For example one piece of Art homework was to use pen and ink to draw 'A view from a window'.

I chose to draw the view from my parents' bedroom which included the playing field and goalposts and the road and houses beyond. I added some flying birds and a small aeroplane. I found drawing difficult, and still do, but I liked my 'view from a window'.

Miss Stanway was pleased with my efforts, but she slipped in a little comment that I could have put more texture into the playing field pitch. I replied indignantly with, 'But I drew what I saw,' and she nodded quietly and moved on to somebody else. The moment I was home I ran upstairs and looked out of the same window. She was right! There was masses of texture in the pitch and the houses opposite. I remember feeling cross with myself and the picture. I still have it, and when I look at it now it makes me smile.

***

We had to carry substantial loads of books to and from school, especially at weekends, and it must have been about this time my school satchel started splitting at the seams. It was repaired a couple of times but I got fed up with it. Army type rucksacks were becoming the 'cool' school accessory and I decided to buy one. When full, it was worn like a rucksack with the straps over both shoulders, but when it held less it could be casually slung over one shoulder.

I continued to enjoy reading and we were given a list of books the school expected us to read out of school hours. My reading interests now covered a broader sweep of literature. I had been in the habit of using West Bridgford library, but was now more inclined to go to the school library, which was a haven of peace.

I developed a liking for historical novels. They took me into romantic swashbuckling worlds of the past, packed with handsome men, beautiful women, intrigue and adventure. C.S Forster's stories of *Horatio Hornblower* had been a favourite with me and then I discovered Georgette Heyer. I was on the school library's waiting list for *Beauvallet* and *Devil's Cub* for ages. When it was my turn to borrow them the books had very well thumbed pages. I was also a fan of the *Biggles* books by W.E.Johns, which are flying adventures, and generally considered to be boys' books. My father's passion must have influenced me.

My interest grew in modern history books such as *The diary of Anne Frank*, which deeply affected me, also, the story of Odette, an ordinary girl, who was sent into enemy territory during the war and died a heroine. The torture she endured made me shudder. Despite being a war baby, I had never properly appreciated before how really horrible war is and that there are some vile people in the world.

On a lighter note, I had discovered magazines which fed my appetite for theatre and film. They were *Plays and Players, Photoplay* and *Film Review*. *Plays and Player*s was the most useful to me as it kept me in touch with what was going on in theatre land.

21

Rock Climbing & Radio Days

It was about this time that I went on a camping and climbing weekend with friends of my parents. They were Alfred and Pat Webster, and their daughters, Anne and Linda, who were younger than me. Alfred was grey haired with a moustache and Pat was glamorous, with wavy reddish hair. We drove to Brassington in the Derbyshire Dales and pulled off the road into a field where we were allowed to set up camp.

I had a small tent to myself and was glad I had had some camping experience with the Guides. I knew how to make myself as comfortable as possible and had a really good torch. It was fantastic fun. Pat and Alf were really kind to me and I helped them with the little girls when I could.

Some other people arrived who were their friends and in the afternoon, armed with coiled ropes and all the other gear climbers need, we set off across the field to the outcrop of rocks which were about five minutes walk away. I have since learned they were the Harborough Rocks, which were well known for being good practice for beginners as well as experienced climbers.

The countryside was beautiful, the rocks were huge and high and I was thrilled to be doing something so adult. Once we arrived, those that were going to climb high, kitted themselves out, and the most nimble and experienced man climbed to the top without any aid. He dropped a rope down for the others to hitch themselves to. If they fell, the rope would save them as the first climber had fixed it at the top. Alf told me to practice on some of the smaller rocks and gave me hints about looking for handholds and never using my knees as support. It was terrific fun, but once I got the hang of it I really wanted to go to the top of one of the taller rocks.

I learned another good lesson that day. One of the other climbers was determined to climb to the top of the rock face without any support. He was half way up when he could not find a new hand or foot hold so he was stuck. Others watching him called out advice, but his legs suddenly started shaking and he let go and fell to the ground. He was not badly hurt but Alf said he would probably be very bruised the next day.

Apart from that, we had a lovely afternoon and went back to camp and had supper. Later, in my tent, I snuggled down in my sleeping bag and fell into a deep sleep.

The next morning Alf asked me if I would like to try going to the top on a rope and I said 'Yes, please!' So, after breakfast we went back with the others and I actually made it to the top with the help of the man ahead of me, who told me where to look for hand and footholds.

It was on that same trip we visited nearby Tissington, where it was 'Well Dressing Weekend.' Every year the villagers decorate their five wells with flowers to make intricate tableaux. There are several theories as to when the tradition started and they are all to give thanks to the wells for protecting the village from disease and drought. The pictures are exquisite - but of course the flowers soon fade.

***

Life at home went on much the same, except that I spent more time in my room doing homework and was becoming aware of the need for my own space away from my brothers. Michael would have been about nine now and Robert four. It still riled me that they were never expected to help around the house.

Well, Robert was still a bit young. But I was so fed up with drying the dishes after lunch or supper that I took to refusing the soup course so there would be one large plate less to dry, which now sounds really pathetic.

I had always had dreams of flying, not in aeroplanes, but under my own volition. In my dreams I would start with a little jump off the ground and then making a pedalling motion. By continuing the pedalling I was able to slowly climb high up into the sky, then fly around, looking at the tiny places and people far below. Sometimes I even flew above the clouds. This must have had something to do with flying with Dad, but I later learned in psychology at college that flying dreams are common in firstborn children. We are trying to get away, far and above our siblings.

I also had strange fantasies or daydreams before and after I dropped off to sleep. These involved me being in some kind of accident and the ambulance people being so gentle and careful with me; wrapping me up to keep me warm and reassuring me that everything was going to be all right. So what would today's shrinks make of that?

***

The wireless, which we now sometimes called the radio, continued to play a significant part in our lives. There were three channels, The Light programme, which broadcast mainly entertainment and music, The Home service, which was more serious and broadcast news and current affairs, and the Third programme which was more serious, and broadcast classical music but, in fact, there was speech, drama and music on all of them.

Saturday lunchtimes in the summer are most memorable to me. Picture the scene. In the kitchen, Mum and Big Granny are busy, one cooking, the other pottering about, and me laying the table. All of the windows are open and there is a test match on the wireless.

There is a gentlemanly commentary, until something 'exciting' happens, and the gentleman becomes louder and more animated, then calms down again; there is the odd smattering of applause and very occasionally, some faint cheers. The broadcast could be coming from the Trent Bridge cricket ground down the road which made it seem like a private broadcast just for us and our neighbours.

John Arlott is a name I remember. I think it was he who, in the middle of a very slow match, mentioned the pigeons wandering on to the pitch – as though they were the only moving things worth watching.

On Saturday evenings, among other programmes, we listened to *Variety Bandbox* and also, *In Town Tonight* which had a very atmospheric beginning. You could hear traffic and a flower seller calling 'violets, luverly sweet violets' . Then a commanding voice said *'Once more we stop the mighty roar of London's traffic and from the great crowds we bring to the microphone some of the interesting people who are 'In Town Tonight."*

The show that followed was just that, not all famous people, but some that just happened to be 'in town tonight'. At the end of the programme, the voice said, '*Carry on London*' and it did! The signature music was wonderful, it was Eric Coates's *Knightsbridge March.*

On Sunday lunchtime, the *Billy Cotton Band Show* began with him shouting, 'Wakey, Wakeeee!' which always got our attention. There were several songs and some silly sketches. *Educating Archie* was another show I loved. It was a comedy, starring a ventriloquist called Peter Brough and his dummy, Archie, who was dressed in a schoolboy's uniform which, of course, we could not see except in photographs in the Radio Times.

I did not think about it at the time, but it now seems strange to broadcast a radio show starring a ventriloquist's dummy! As a point of interest, I have discovered that many people in *Educating Archie* were to become famous. Tony Hancock was Archie's first tutor; others were Benny Hill, Harry Secombe, Dick Emery, Bernard Bresslaw, Hattie Jacques, Bruce Forsyth and Max Bygraves. A young Julie Andrews played his girlfriend and she was followed by Beryl Reid.

For the other comedy programmes I enjoyed, see **Radio Comedy** at the back of the book

Later on a Sunday afternoon, if I heard the *Carousel Waltz* by Richard Rogers playing, I knew that *Movie-go-Round* was about to begin. I would rush to hear it as it had all the news and clips from current films.

As well as the comedy and entertainment programmes there were also drama series broadcast in the early evening: *Riders of the Range, 1943-55.* I can still recall the *'kerching kerching'* of spurs and saddles as they galloped across the prairie. Charles Chilton wrote these and also followed up with the brilliant *Journey into Space.* I really enjoyed *Riders of the Range*, but *Journey into Space* was something else. It was exactly what the title says. There were three main characters: Captain Jet Morgan, Lemmy and Doc. With titles such as: *Operation Lunar, The Red Planet* and *The World in Peril* it could not go wrong!

I used to sit close to the radio in the front room when it was on. I can remember being totally gripped by the series, but any details of what gripped me is now hidden away in the dimmest recesses of my memory.

We must have become a house of many radios; Dad had one in his office,

Mum had one on the window ledge in the kitchen, there was a large one in the front room, which Big Granny also listened to and by now I had my own, which was quite bulky but after 'permitted hours' could be listened to under the bedclothes. Mine ran on batteries so there was no chance of getting an electric shock.

Twenty Questions was another programme we enjoyed. This was a game where a four panellists had to guess a secret object by asking twenty questions - and no more. The chairman could answer only yes or no to their questions. It could be very funny because we at home knew what the object was, as the mystery voice had already told us. The panel always started by asking if the object was animal, vegetable or mineral.

Mum especially liked *Letter from America* by Alistair Cooke. He had moved to America and this programme was just fifteen minutes of him talking about his observations of events and life there. I did not always understand everything he said, but he had a kind voice and he sometimes made Mum laugh.

Any Questions started when I was about seven years old. It was very similar to today's version, where there is chairperson and a panel of four people, often including a couple of politicians. Members of the audience had prepared questions that they read out. Sometimes a member of the panel could get very annoyed if another disagreed with them. Alternatively, it could be very amusing - one response I particularly remember was when the question was something like :

'What can we do about the litter everywhere and how should litter louts be punished?'

One man on the panel answered very fiercely:

'Put them in the stocks, sir, and pelt them with their own rubbish!' which I thought was hilarious.

I was keen on drama and radio was an excellent medium for plays, although some of them were on late at night. *Under Milk Wood* with Richard Burton was first broadcast in 1954 and I heard it. I was thrilled to hear him on the radio.

I also remember the BBC's S.O.S. Messages. When there was a dire emergency and people needed to be contacted, these were read in between programmes. For example:

'And now an urgent SOS message: would Mr John Smith, last heard of in the area of Winchester, please contact Birmingham General Hospital on telephone no: .... where his mother, Elsie Smith is dangerously ill.'

I sometimes wondered what happened next. Did Mr Smith hear the message? Did one of his friends hear it? Did he have a brother or sister who heard it? Did he see his mother in time? Why had he lost contact with his mother - or couldn't they find her address book? Did she have an address book? It all remained a mystery to me.

We children may have moaned about not having a television, but the radio kept us amused for much of our leisure time at home. We still played board games and I also had books and my record player. I do not recall every being bored.

Michael at some point, began violin lessons with excruciating results - poor brother, I was not very kind to him about his playing. Mum played the piano, although her repertoire was limited, and she had little time to practice, I especially remember her playing *Fur Elise* by Beethoven, and Chopin's *Minute Waltz*. I still have a book of the sheet music she used. Her playing always sounded lovely.

***

In the Summer term Drama Competition, my class entered a production of scenes from *Tobias and The Angel* by James Bridie. I was the producer and it was really good fun. With my sewing machine skills I was also able to make several pairs of baggy trousers for the Eastern girls. To my huge disappointment, just before we were due to perform, I caught the flu and was too ill to go to school. Fortunately one of my friends stood in for me (Susan Chapman I was so grateful to you!). And we won. Here is how it was reported in the school magazine:

.....This was followed by UIVD's Tobias and the Angel; when the curtains went back on the set of this it was greeted with a gasp, for this enterprising Form appeared to have transported whole trees to the stage to create an Eastern garden. Closer inspection revealed a fountain that really

worked and the appearance of a live dog on the stage half way through the play completed the realism of the scene. Great attention had been paid, too, to the grouping and rehearsing of the minor characters, so the unfortunate absence of both the producer and the main character, Tobias, during the previous week were triumphantly overcome and the Form deservedly won the shield.

***

Away from school and wandering further from home, we sometimes met up with new friends, notably a couple of local youths who went to the boys' high school. Their school was known as 'THE High School' because there was a time, that lasted for at least 500 years, when it was the only high school in Nottingham. However, in 2015, they finally admitted girls into the hallowed halls.

I got to know a couple of the boys as I saw them on the bus most mornings and they became friends. We had met before on the sledging hill and now they came with us when we went up into the fields. They showed us other places to explore like the Spinney, which I always thought was a bit spooky and also The Quarry which we had been told not to go near, as it was dangerous, but we were never told how or why.

We took great care walking round it and found a disused crane cabin. It had no roof and was removed from its caterpillar wheels. We climbed inside and tried smoking some disgusting herbal cigarettes which made us cough a lot. (They were NOT marijuana but some kind of 'health' cigarettes). However the worst time was when we insanely started a small fire in the cabin and nearly all choked to death. The smoke did not escape as we had planned, but gusted in circles all round the cab, causing total panic as we clambered to the top of the walls, where we hung gasping and spluttering in the fresh air, tears pouring down our cheeks. We never returned and told no one.

However, adventures aside, school was about to become more demanding. Next term saw the first of two years of preparation for our G.C.E. O Level Exams. Life was beginning to get more serious.

22

Games & Pets

I have already mentioned some of the games we played in break times, but in the Upper Third, three of us, dark-haired Kay Fowler, with twinkly eyes, Ruth Howard, who wore a parting in her straight fair hair and myself played ball games against a windowless wall.

The basis of the game was to throw the ball at the wall in different ways and to catch it on its return before it bounced on the ground. The sequence, played by one girl at a time, was something like:

1. Underarm throw and catch.
2. Under one leg throw and catch.
3. Under the other leg throw and catch.
4. Round the back throw and catch.
5. Throw the ball and turn round on the spot in time to catch it.

We then speeded it up by doubling up on each throw, or bouncing the ball on the ground before it hit the wall, or trying to throw with our backs to the wall, all sorts of varieties, and number 5 could become became particularly tricky.

In the playground we still played the old favourites including Hot Rice, which had been temporarily banned, until it was agreed the ball would never be aimed at the head of the person being chased.

The games we played as part of the school curriculum were Rounders, Netball, Hockey and Tennis. In the 2nd form, when we played Rounders, I played Backstop, the position I liked best.

I was never much good at games but I enjoyed playing them. The playgrounds at the back of the school doubled up as netball courts in the winter and tennis courts in the summer. Once we started playing hockey we had to take a short bus ride to the school playing field on Thackeray's Lane, where there were tennis courts and a hockey pitch. It was also where the school sports day was held. I once cart wheeled across the whole pitch but I cannot remember why.

I have only hazy memories of sports days. I was not the best runner, but was tolerably good at the high and long jump. I was also good at throwing things, especially the cricket ball and later the javelin. However, one of my enduring memories is of a girl who was a whizz at the sack race.

Anne Hacking was pretty, blonde and short, so short, in fact, that while everyone else was lolloping and jumping along in their sacks, Anne had stuck a foot in each of the corners of her sack, and ran like the wind to the other end of the course - winning by miles. She did it every year and always received a huge round of applause from the spectators.

Another time, on a hot Summer's afternoon, after playing tennis on the field courts we were all gathered around the pavilion having drinks and snacks when Kay shrieked and shouted 'I've been stung!'

She had been sharing an apple with a wasp which had stung her tongue. There was staff consternation over whether Kay could have swallowed the wasp. Someone said they had seen one on the ground but we could not find it anywhere, so one of the teachers drove Kay to hospital. Kay was fine the next day, but since then I have always checked the other side of a piece of fruit before biting into it, especially apples.

In Netball I usually played Centre, or on one of the wings. Kay was a skilful goal shooter. We used to have some terrific games. I was once coerced to play for the school in a match on a Saturday morning because they were desperate for a reserve team member. We lost, but not too badly.

Hockey provided me physically with the most uncomfortable afternoons of my schooldays and one of the most humiliating experiences.

The latter was a disastrous hockey match when I was in the Upper Thirds. Our games teacher, Miss Glossop, had quickly put a team together to play St Joseph's. It was a cold, dull muddy day and none of us had any previous experience of playing in a school match.

We had been strictly trained not to wander across the field but to keep our positions, passing to each other at the right moment once we had possession of the ball. I played Left Wing. The whistle blew, the Centre Forwards bullied off, St Joseph's got the ball, passed it very quickly, and then, apart from their goalkeeper, their whole team, like a swarm of bees, gathered around the ball moving it across the pitch all the way to our goal.

That was how they scored the first goal - and several more. After half time and we had changed ends they did exactly the same thing. I do not think I ever touched the ball. The final score was 10 - 2. So much for playing by the rules.

I saw our games teacher smiling to herself and shaking her head at the end of the game. We were mortified when the score was read out in Morning Assembly. Looking back now it reads like a plot worthy of St Trinian's.

The most physically uncomfortable afternoons were after we moved to the new playing fields. I must have been in the Upper 5 or Lower 6. Not only were they a much longer bus journey away, but they seemed unfriendly wide open spaces, not like our smaller cosier 'old' field. Playing on the wing in howling freezing winds did not endear me to the game of hockey at all.

Then 'they' expected us to go and shower in a COMMUNAL SHOWER! There had been no showers at the old field on Thackeray's Lane and apart from sharing a cubicle with a friend at the swimming pool, most of us had never seen each other naked.

One or two freer souls showered together, but the rest of us shy little wimps, just rubbed off any mud and changed in the dressing rooms. Anyway, we could not have been very sweaty, it was too blinking cold on the field to perspire even one drip. Not surprisingly, the new playing fields became known as 'Siberia'.

***

My first pet was a tortoise. I really liked it. I loved to see him put his head out of his shell and slowly munch through a leaf. I was pretty sure it was a 'him', but I could not think of a name for ages. He ended up being called No-Name. In the garden I marked off a small area with low wire netting for No-Name to move around in. I also made him a house out of an upturned wooden box with a wide doorway cut out of one of the sides. I painted 'No-Name' over the doorway. He was regularly fed on a variety of soft leaves and there was always a shallow bowl of water for him, but I never saw him drink out of it.

We were told that the only problem with tortoises was that they hibernate. So, I made No-Name a special hibernating box filled with straw. However, he was not in the least interested in it and remained wide awake. Winter was approaching, and to be on the safe side we brought him into the loggia where it was much warmer than outside, and hoped he would survive in the straw filled box - or out of it.

Luckily No-Name was fine and continued to be so until one summer, after a storm, I went down the garden to check he was all right. He was lying on his front outside his little house; his head was on one side and his legs splayed outside his shell. He showed no sign of life. I called my mother and she came and was very comforting. We buried him in the garden with a stone to mark where he lay.

I was in the Lower Thirds, Miss Wilmot's class when this happened and I clearly remember telling her. It was very odd, I was upset about No–Name dying but when I told Miss Wilmot and she was sympathetic I felt an unreasonable urge to smile, but I reallydid not want to. It was a weird confusion. My being sad was mixed up with not wanting to make her sad too. I appreciated her sympathy and therefore I had to smile to show her I was all right.

I kept goldfish for several years - two at first. Their bowl was in my bedroom and at night I could hear them making little plip plip noises when they came to the surface. At first they were in a bowl, but it was not the type with a narrow neck; it was more of a hexagonal shape. I put some oxygenating weed in it and changed the water regularly, leaving it to stand for a while so it was the same temperature as the one the fish were used to.

Later, I bought a bigger tank and some more goldfish friends. I found them fascinating. They lived for quite a long time, although I do remember one death. I found a motionless fish on its side, floating near the surface of the water. It was also buried in the garden with a smaller stone than No–Name to mark its grave. I also kept some rabbits - two brown ones; they were not very tame and inclined to nip or kick and I think Dad gave them to someone at the flying club.

Then, when I was in the Upper Fourth, a new girl asked me if I would like some guinea pigs as hers kept having babies and she had too many. I asked Mum and Dad and they said it should be all right. So I acquired two guinea pigs.

They were very pretty but not very tame - one was black and white and the other, ginger, black and white. They could make quite a racket, a sort of chuntering and squealing, or a growly purring. However, after a few weeks I was shocked to find some dead babies in their run.

Mum thought that one of them had been pregnant when we were given them and she was not too pleased. The adults were very healthy, and we eventually gave them away to somebody who a had bigger run.

My brother Michael had a white rat which he called Snowy. Snowy was a lovely pet, very tame and friendly. He had amazing glittery red eyes. One day he became very lethargic and unresponsive and lay still for what seemed ages. I noticed a wasp in his run and we guessed he had been stung by it. Fortunately Snowy made a full recovery.

After Monty died, we did not have a cat for a while. Maybe my mother decided we needed one after the 'mouse in the dressing up box' incident. There was Ginger, and then later on, Snowy who was around until well after I left school.

We caught and kept tadpoles in large jam jars and later put them in a friend's pond - although thinking back now, we had a tiny pond of our own for a while. I recall occasionally seeing a frog there and even a newt. Also in the days before the lawn was planted there were plenty of muddy patches and puddles to attract them.

I think our parents must have been fairly easy going about pets as I do not remember any family rows about them. Apart from the goldfish they were always kept in the loggia or in the garage at the bottom of the garden. I once painted a view of the garden from my bedroom window. On the left hand side of the picture you can just see the school we watched being built, and apart from the houses in the far distance, there were fields and wasteland all around us until the nearby houses were built.

140.

23

Flying with Dad

My Dad loved flying. That is basically the long and short of my Dad. He had always loved flying. In the 1930's there was not only a shortage of Royal Air Force pilots, but also a fear that another war was inevitable. Dad, who was working at Permutit, joined the Auxiliary Air Force and was able to take advantage of Air Marshall Dowding's strategy to recruit pilots by subsidising their training.

Dad not only acquired his pilot's licence, but also an instructor's licence and left his job at Permutit for a full time post in the Royal Air Force Volunteer Reserve. During the war he met Mum at her mother's boarding house in Kew and his diary at the time was nothing short of cryptic:

26th April 1940
Since last writing
I have become engaged
I have crashed.

The crash was in the previous October when he and a pupil managed to fly into a tree.

On June 7th 1940 he and Mum were married and he continued to instruct pilots throughout the war years. He was so committed to his duties that he was awarded the Distinguished Flying Medal for his record number of instructing hours. He even went to Buckingham Palace to be presented with it by King George VIth. He rarely talked about the war and I never really appreciated what he had gone through in those terrible years. It must have been a great sadness to him that so many of the young men he trained to fly had died in combat.

After the joy and celebrations at the end of war it must have been a harsh wrench for him to leave full time flying and return to his job with Permutit.

When we moved to Nottingham, he began to train pilots again at weekends. The proximity of several airfields and the growing demand for flying instruction by civilian pilots, was of some consolation to him.

For a while, we children were lucky enough to be included in his flying activities. This was not just in the making of kites or model aeroplanes; he took us flying in light aircraft as soon as we were sensible enough to know how to behave in one.

From the very beginning of my remembering anything, we were never far from an airfield. I described some of this in the first chapter. After the war, if we were travelling in the car and passed an airfield, Dad would invariably drive in to take a look around. Also, if we were driving somewhere he always gave a lift to a service man thumbing a ride.

Mum told me that she and Dad once hoped they might find an airfield where he could teach people to fly and she would run a little cafe. This was never to happen, but Dad gradually spent more of his Saturdays and Sundays away from home teaching people and enjoying the company of other flying enthusiasts.

I have memories of cold and foggy Sunday afternoons when Dad took Michael and me to Tollerton airfield. There were some old aeroplanes parked there which we were allowed to climb over and sit in the cockpit. Michael has since told me they were three Lancaster Bombers and an abandoned Harvard. However my most clear memories of airfields and aeroplanes are of when Dad took me to Burnaston Airfield - later known as Derby Airport. It had been an RAF training school since before the war and when we moved to Nottingham he first trained some cadets there. I remember seeing some in their uniforms.

There was also a flying club where there was no shortage of aspiring civilian pilots who were willing to pay quite a lot of money for flying lessons. Mum told me that Dad particularly liked taking people up for their very first flying lessons. He later became an examiner and eventually he became an examiner's examiner!

At Burnaston I spent most of my time watching the small aeroplanes taking off and landing and once the staff knew me, I was allowed to wander around the hangar to look at the planes, but certainly not to climb over them.

142.

I learnt that you never, never touched a propeller, in fact the advice was to always give them a wide berth. I loved going into the hangar and seeing the planes silently waiting. It was a huge airy space and often smelled strongly of the dope which they painted on to the fabric of the planes.

When the weather was cold or not so good for flying we stayed inside the office. From there you could see what was happening on and above the airfield. With luck, most times I accompanied Dad he would get us a flight - either with one of his qualified pupils or he would take me up on his own. We often flew in an Auster. The wing was above the cockpit and there were two seats at the front for the pilot and passenger, or two pilots. I sat in the back which was a bit squashed but I could see everything.

My father was always meticulous. He would first walk around the plane to check everything looked as it should. In the cockpit, immediately above the windscreen he had fixed a row of handwritten capital letters, a mnemonic for the pre-flight checks for the aircraft. He always quietly insisted both pilots, he being one of them, went through the same checks. Then the propeller would be turned and the engine leapt into life and we taxied, bump, bump, bump, across the field and turned to face whichever direction was best for take-off into the wind.

Final checks were made, the engine revved a little and we moved forward, steadily gaining speed - then less bumpy but more rattling along and then, up and away and suddenly everything was smooth and quiet, apart from the sound of the engine. As the plane climbed the land dropped away and the world below became smaller and smaller, turning into a model of itself. Sometimes we flew through low cloud, which for the first time for me, was very exciting.

Eventually the time came to return to the airfield and after checking there were no other planes in the area, Dad lined up the plane for landing. At first our descent seemed slow and quite wobbly. Then when we were almost down I could see from the way we whizzed past the trees and houses we were still moving fast.

We slowed down more, until with a bump we were on the ground. The plane trundled across the field to park near the hangar where we stopped, the engine was turned off and the propeller came to rest.

I especially liked going up in an aircraft called the Miles Magister. This was also a small light plane with two cockpits above the wing, one behind the other and open to the elements. I had to wear a leather helmet and a warm jacket and was strapped in tight. If there was some low cloud around and we flew above it, the world below would vanish and it was as though we were the only people in the air above the earth: just the sound of the engine and Dad and me in misty white world.

I enjoyed going to the airfield. There was always something going on. Sometimes a larger aeroplane called a Rapide would arrive from Jersey with passengers on board. It was a blue green colour and looked like a coach with two wings propped up on two large front wheels. Later a Dakota was in service,

I got to know some of Dad's pupils. The talk was always of aeroplanes and flights and the weather. They were always very jolly and friendly. Unfortunately though, flying is a dangerous business and our days there were not without incident. Once, an air show was held with all sorts of events. The RAF cadets were on duty to help organise things and we were all there as well: Dad, Mum, Michael, Robert, who was still quite young, and me.

There was a race; the contestants had to fly around a course designated by three church towers. The pilots set off according to their handicaps and were timed individually. It was not much of spectator sport because we depended on the public address system to know what was going on.

I cannot remember much else of the afternoon except for a game when a certain number of balloons were released over the airfield and the pilots took it in turns to see how many they could burst. One of them changed direction in a steep turn, went into a stall too low to be safe, could not pull out, and smashed into the ground with a terrible crunching sound.

The plane immediately caught fire. Thankfully, this happened a good distance away from we spectators and there was a shocked silence pierced by Robert, shouting 'Daddy! Daddy!' and the clanging and roaring engines of the Emergency Services racing to the crash, followed by air cadets running over to see if they could help.

In my head was disbelief, but in my heart I felt the pilot could not have survived. It was so sudden, so immediate, an exploding matchbox, the flames already dying down and dark smoke rising into the sky. Robert was consoled the moment he could see Dad. My mother never went to an airfield again.

***

My father was an ace at aerobatics. Sometimes he was asked to fly at air shows. When he could he would use a Tiger Moth and it was marvellous to see; loops, rolls off the top, stalling and falling and pulling out; it all took my breath away.

As it so happened, my breath was also taken away once when Dad took me up in a Miles Magister. It was a Sunday - I know because I had fainted (yes I was still fainting) in church at communion, but when I got home and told my parents he whisked me off for some fresh air at the airfield and off we went in the red Magister.

The air felt fantastic up there. We had been climbing for a few minutes when he spoke through the intercom and asked me how I was feeling. I said I felt fine and he said, 'Hold on then,' and we went into a dive, pulled out and swooped up again and over the top (that is when he took my breath away) - we had looped the loop!

He asked me if I was still fine and I shouted, 'Yes!' and laughed. So I now had the reputation as the girl who fainted in church and by elevenses had looped the loop with her Dad. It felt wonderful.

24

Singing & *Dancing*
Lower 5L September 1955-September 1956

In the Lower Fifth we knew at some point we were going to have to decide which subjects to take at O. Level. I continued studying Latin until the end of the Lower Fifth year. I know this because I have a certificate from school which says so. There was a rhyme going round at the time:

Latin is a language, as dead as dead can be,

It killed the ancient Romans, and now it's killing me.

I quite enjoyed Latin and although I dropped it, I am really glad I studied it for as long as I did. I have forgotten much of it, but there have been times when it has been useful. When trying to work out the meaning of an English word there can be a syllable of Latin which has lasted through the centuries and can be a hint, or even a key to the meaning. Latin can also pop up in some European languages and again can be a clue to meaning. Basic Latin can also be useful in deciphering engravings, even on graveyard headstones.

In December 1955, my first term in the Lower Fifth year, the school play was *The Lady's not for Burning* by Christopher Fry, with Miss Gornall producing. It was a senior school production and I was very pleased to be cast as Richard the clerk. Kay was cast as Alizon and she and my character, Richard, fall in love and run away near the end of the play. I was not familiar with Christopher Fry's writing but I loved the script and it was exciting to work with members of the senior school, some of whom were very talented actors.

There was one exit line I have never forgotten; it was the rather bumbling Chaplain who as he left the stage turned and said '*God bless you, in case you sneeze'.*

The audience loved it.

Memories of these two school years are rather vague. I put it down to exam fever, but I think that was the year when we put on scenes from *Pygmalion* for the drama competition. It had a good review but we did not win anything

One subject I have not yet mentioned is the music and singing classes. We had two music teachers, Mrs Moult, who also took us for needlework and Miss Sandy, a smart, younger, more demanding teacher who certainly got results. Miss Sandy had a piercing voice when giving instructions over us trying to follow a tune. In earlier days we had had some music theory lessons and I learned the basic rudiments of musical notes and timing. Although I was never reduced to being a 'growler' by Miss Sandy, I was never selected for the choir.

It was Miss Sandy's responsibility to produce the school choir's songs at the annual prize giving which took place in the Albert Hall in Nottingham, to us, an impressive Edwardian building. On one or two occasions we all stood up with the choir and joined in. We must have made a powerful sound!

We had singing lessons most of the school years and I remember some of the songs very fondly. There was one I particularly liked with lyrics something like:

Brave isle of meadow, cliff and cloud, where windflower hope
forever blows'

I have never been able to trace it, even with the easy access to information the internet provides these days. Another jollier song went:

Said Oliver Cromwell if you please
Don't doff your bonnet or bend your knees
Don't offer me sceptre robe or ring
*For Oliver Cromwell won't be Kin*g

And another :

'A flaxen headed cowboy as handsome as may be
A flaxen headed cowboy, who wandered o'er the lea'

I enjoyed singing in class and at prize giving in the Albert Hall, but especially when we all sang carols together in Morning Assembly as Christmas approached .

***

It was about this time that I joined the Portland Baths Swimming Club. Meetings took place on Friday evenings and there were special times for swimmers to race up and down the pool. I caught the 24 bus, and it only took ten minutes to get there. The baths were on Muskham Street, off Arkwright Street, where the bus stopped. The changing rooms were dark brown wooden cubicles around the pool, men on one side women on the other. In each cubicle there were hooks to hang up clothes and towels, and a small bench.

I always tried to avoid the cubicles near the deep end of the pool as people diving off the boards sometimes made huge splashes. If the water came over the sides of the nearby cubicles you ended up with soggy towels and clothes to go home in.

I enjoyed the whole sensation of diving in and swimming through the water as I still do today. I was always starving when I came out, but had been forbidden by my father to buy chips and eat them on the bus home. It was not considered good behaviour in public.

At home, things were slightly different, I was becoming more independent and my social circle was changing. On Saturday afternoons I started catching a bus to a village just outside West Bridgford for ballroom dancing lessons. They were held in Burnside Hall, Plumtree, and they were terrific fun. Girls and boys came from all around. Sheila from my road came, as well as other girls I knew through the Guides.

The classes were run by a inspiring blonde woman who was very jolly, but strict about us executing the correct moves. We learned all the classic steps: *Waltz, Quickstep, Foxtrot, Tango, Polka* and the traditional old time *Gay Gordons, Valeta, Military Two Step, Boston two step* - and of course, the *Conga* and the *Barn Dance*.

During each of the classes we were allowed to make a request for a particular dance and this is how I learned a rather perilous one called *the Basket*. A group who had been attending the classes for longer always requested it so our teacher was obliged to instruct the rest of us.

The Basket started with couples forming a circle facing into the centre, boy, girl, boy, girl. There were some opening two step movements, then

148.

the boys all joined hands behind the girls and the girls all joined hands behind the boys until everyone's arms were interlaced. The whole circle went round and round, faster and faster, until all the girls' feet lifted off the ground behind them and they flew round. It was fantastic.

We all laughed and screamed while we held on tight until the boys slowed down and our feet touched the floor again. If anyone let go, girls could get flung across the room. In the end our teacher banned *the Basket* as she was worried someone was going to be badly hurt.

Suddenly the world of teenagers changed dramatically. *'Rock around the Clock'* by Bill Haley and the Comcts burst upon us and was constantly played on the radio. Rock and Roll was here to stay, so we were taught how to jive properly and do all the more acrobatic moves – if we felt like it. They were quite dangerous too.

I had a special favourite outfit for those afternoons. It consisted of a fine knit orange jumper and a circular skirt with a frill at the hem which came to below my knees. It was not a frilly frill - more like an extra, slightly wider, piece of fabric which gave the skirt more weight to spin out. It was blue with black splodges. Underneath it I wore a paper nylon underskirt which I rinsed in sugared water and then drip dried. The sugar solution made it stiffer in order to hold the skirt out.

I had very little jewellery and my ears were not yet pierced. I found clip-on earrings excruciatingly uncomfortable and only put them on when I arrived at the hall and took them off the moment I left. I had some poppet beads I used to wear round my neck. They were plastic beads which popped together or apart so you could alter the length of the necklace - or bracelet. I made a small necklace to go around the neck of my jumper.

In winter time I wore a roll-on with built in suspenders to hold up my stockings. A roll-on was a wide tube of elasticated material pulled over your waist and hips, which helped to hold your tummy in and stockings up, at the same time helping to keep you warm. In the summer, though, a roll on would be discarded for a suspender belt, or, when it was hot, short white socks instead of stockings.

Stockings were made of nylon and 30 or 15 denier in texture; 30 being thicker - and therefore stronger; 15 being thin and easy to catch on anything that had a rough edge. Annoyingly, fingernails or toenails could easily catch when pulling on a stocking. This often caused a ladder which could 'run' all the way from the caught thread to the top or foot of the stocking. The best thing to stop the ladder 'running,' was a dab of clear nail varnish which made the repair almost invisible. Stockings could have a seam at the back which had to be kept straight, but most of us took to wearing seamless stockings, which saved endless checking and fiddling around to keep them straight. Little did we realise that within a few years roll-ons & suspender belts would be history and girls would enjoy the freedom of tights.

Since playing Richard in the school play I had decided to grow my hair again. I could not wait to have a pony tail as I really liked Brigitte Bardot's hairstyle.

I was not particularly interested in boys at the time of going to the dance classes. The boys I went up in the fields with were more like friends or brothers. But I loved the dancing at Burnside Hall, especially with a boy called Richard because he was such a good dancer. He was very nice and good fun, but he was just not tall enough for my liking. There were several other boys there too; I had a bit of a crush on another one but he already had a girlfriend.

Towards the end of my time there, some of the boys, including Richard, formed a skiffle group and they were very good. I took photos of them with my flash camera. Our teacher let them play at one of our dance party evenings, everybody loved it, and we all clapped and screamed like mad. They were very happy times.

***

We were all growing up. I was young for my school year and most of my contemporaries were already wearing bras. I eventually ask Mum about it. She said if I felt I needed one she would come with me to help me make the right selection. I was very relieved about this. We had a trip up to town to Jessops, a large department store with a lingerie department. Mum told me it was very important to be measured to find a bra that fitted properly and I still follow her advice.

My first period arrived on a freezing cold winter's evening after a dancing lesson at Burnside Hall. I was no stranger to stomach aches and cramps and I had had some all day. These turned out to be for something different when I found I had what looked like some smears of blood on my blue school knickers. I told Mum and she showed me how to use sanitary towels which first made me feel I was walking with an elephant between my legs.

I soon became used to them and despite the whole thing being a massive nuisance when it came to swimming, I rarely suffered from the pre menstrual pain and symptoms which some of my friends experienced. Eventually using tampons solved the swimming problem.

The other medical excitement I had was a verucca. It looked like a small black spot under my foot and was painful. Mum had to take me to a special verucca clinic in the City where I had dry ice pressed firmly on to it which stung like mad and was painful for hours.

The dry ice burned and formed a blister with the verucca on top. Over a few weeks I had to scrape the top skin off until the verucca had gone entirely. I could hardly walk on it when we came out of the clinic and Mum felt so sorry for me she relented her stand about my having anything remotely resembling a high heel.

She bought me a pretty pair of shoes in pale brown, a sort of mushroomy coloured suede with small high heels, which I adored. Once the stinging pain had gone and the skin under my foot had settled down I devoted some time every two or three days to paring the skin off with my Airfix balsa wood knife.

My First Aid training in the Guides had taught me emergency sterilising principles and I poured boiling water over the blade before I used it. It was a perfect tool for the task and when Mum took me back to the clinic they were delighted with my new skin. But they looked somewhat askance when I told them how I got rid of it. From that day on I was always very careful at swimming pools, often wearing flip flops or light beach shoes. But my new shoes were an absolute dream.

The other dancing venue I now went to was the Palais de Danse in Nottingham - usually known as 'The Pally'. These classes were on Saturday mornings in the ballroom, which was a lovely space to dance in. There was a mirror ball and it was all a bit grand. We had a break in the middle of the morning and that was the first time I heard *Little Blue Riding Hood*, a Stan Freeberg spoof of the *Dragnet* series. I thought it was hilarious.

These Saturday mornings were fun, especially when a whole row of us were dancing the Palais Glide. We used to dance it to *Side by side*, singing:

Oh we ain't got a barrel of money
Maybe we're ragged and funny
But we'll travel along
Singing a song side by side

Don't know what's comin' tomorrow
Maybe it's trouble and sorrow
But we'll travel the road
Sharing our load side by side

Through all kinds of weather
What if the sky should fall
Just as long as we're together
It doesn't matter at all

When they've all had their quarrels and parted
We'll be the same as we started
Just a-travelling along
Singing a song side by side

I have rarely danced it since and have quite forgotten the steps. On Saturday afternoons tea dances were held at the Palais. I went to a couple and a band played which made it more atmospheric but it was never as jolly as Burnside Hall.

25

Being a Teenager
Upper 5R September 1956-September 1957

Closer to home, I continued to join 'the gang' in the fields and the woods. Myxomatosis had spread everywhere, and we saw little rabbits tottering around in the woodland, suffering from the disease. Two of the boys had powerful air rifles, which they took to bringing with them and putting the rabbits out of their misery.

It was a horrible thing to do but we felt it was right. I had no idea what the guns laws were then - but it did not occur to me that what we were doing might be illegal. The boys were in the Combined Cadet Force at school and knew how to take good care when they were handling their air rifles.

However, I did not mention any of this to my parents, and having seen the diseased rabbits, it was a great relief to me that my mother stopped making rabbit pie.

It was about this time a family insurance policy matured and Mum said I could have it for a new carpet and curtains in my bedroom. I chose a navy carpet with coloured geometric shapes and my curtains were a light bluey grey with lines and coloured abstract shapes. It was all very modern.

My father stuck his head around the door to have a look and his comment was, 'Mmm - yes the carpet's a bit small,' but I was past caring what he thought then. I thought it was really cool. The other features in my bedroom were a dressing table, a wardrobe, a funny wooden chair - its back curved round to form arms, a tall, narrow built-in cupboard and a desk I had made myself.

I painted it a cream colour. The desk looked a bit clunky. It had a lid with a compartment below to keep books. Sadly, it was badly designed, so the bottom kept falling out and the books tumbled to the floor, but as a practical surface for writing on it was fine.

When I was learning quotations and translations off by heart I always sat on my new carpet, where I consumed many tubes of Rowntree's fruit gums to help me concentrate. My room was never tidy, there were books, paints and papers everywhere and sometimes clothes all over the floor.

Mum threatened to put everything left on the floor under my bedclothes, but she never did. Not like the mother of a friend of mine who made her an apple pie bed and put all her stuff down it.

My bed was sprung metal with a wooden bed head. There was also a hanging light switch which controlled the light above. This switch was egg shaped and I used to mess around with it, swinging it around and catching it. Sometimes it became loose and I gave myself several shocks when I fiddled with it and it fell apart. It is amazing I am still alive. I kept my record player on the floor with my portable radio.

I loved my portable radio, I could not only tune into late evening dramas on the Third programme, but also to music on Radio Luxembourg. This was commercially run and known as a 'Pirate' radio station. The signal for Radio Luxembourg was not always reliable, but when it was strong it was wonderful to hear the music. At 11pm on Sundays many a teenager's ear would be held close to a radio to hear the Top Twenty tunes of the week.

The programmes were interspersed by commercials which seemed to go on forever. A memorable one was a man called Horace Bachelor promoting his 'Infra draw' method, which he claimed increased chances of winning large amounts on the football pools.

Listeners were asked to submit their stakes to him at Department One, Keynsham, spelt K-E-Y-N-S-H-A-M, Keynsham, Bristol. I still remember it well - and how to spell it.

***

Guy Fawkes night became more exciting; we helped the younger children make guys but, looking back, we did dreadful things with *Little Demons* or *Thunderflashes*, the names of bangers we regularly threw at each other. I once got a *Jumping Jack* caught in the hood of my duffle coat, but luckily it jumped out again and fell to the ground.

I loved the bonfire and the fireworks, especially the Catherine Wheels

154.

and Rockets. It was always an exciting evening for bringing neighbours and friends together.

I was now allowed to help Dad supervise the lighting of the family fireworks. Mum provided sausages, sandwiches and flapjacks, as well as comfort to the younger children who didn't like the bangs. One year I made toffee apples but they were not very successful. The toffee was all right though. As more houses were built around us there was less waste land for bonfires and eventually we gathered around smaller bonfires in our own gardens.

That winter was very harsh. It snowed, then thawed and froze, then-snowed again. The roads and pavements were dangerously icy, but the sledging was great. There was packed snow on the playground and we made slides which were like glass. Really like glass. The school showed huge common sense. Instead of sprinkling salt all over them, which they would have no doubt done today, they allowed them to stay.

Miss Milford addressed the whole school in Assembly about the safe way to use the slides and the games teachers were seconded to be on break duty to show us how to balance and slide sensibly. It was amazing – we could slide for miles as well as holding on to each other in a train, when we often crashed over in a heap.

***

I continued to be actively interested in theatre and drama. I read the magazines, listened to the radio dramas and in the spring of 1956 I was thrilled to go on a school outing to Stratford on Avon to see Shakespeare's *Othello*. Harry Andrews played *Othello*, Emlyn Williams played *Iago* and Margaret Johnston, *Desdemona*.

I was completely overcome and enthralled with the show and just knew I had to join that world. My photographs had become more serious - they were of the exterior of the Stratford Memorial Theatre, a statue of *Falstaff* and some swans by the river.

About this time I also went on a trip with my friend Ann Pearson and her father. They invited me to go with them to Bradford where we would visit a greetings card company and stay the night in a hotel. The trip made several

155.

lasting impressions on me. Ann's father was in packaging and once showed me how a box could be made from one sheet of card, that was shaped, cut and folded, according to the specific need of the product.

Since then I have always been fascinated by how ingenious these designs can be and I have been known to open out a box just to see how one flat piece of card has been adapted.

The visit to the card factory amazed me as well. We saw how the illustrations on the cards gradually emerged as they were printed with additional tints and colours to make up the final picture. I was never before aware of the variety of hues that existed within the palette of the printing process.

The other thing I particularly remember is the hotel room that Ann and I shared. It was large, with a lofty ceiling and everything was very brown. In the similarly lofty bathroom, the bath, sink and lavatory were all a spotless shiny white, except on the top of the cistern there were the biggest black smuts ever. They had floated in from a high window. The air outside must have been really dirty from the industry around the city.

The other event that thrilled me on the trip was going to see *The King and I* in a massive cinema. It was very impressive, and so was the film.

***

My parents had given me an electric record player for Christmas and I was now buying 45rpm records with a track on each side. My collection included: Bill Haley's *Rock around the Clock, Shake rattle and Roll* and *See you later Alligator* and of course, Elvis Presley songs.

I was so excited at having bought the double sided hit of his *Hound Dog* and *Don't be Cruel*, that I took my record player into my father's office when he was out and played it down the phone to my friend Kay. It was one of the few times I saw my mother incandescent with fury. 'You must stop that at once!' she shouted.

'Why?' I asked humming along to *Don't be cruel*.

'Because your father might be expecting a phone call.'

'But he's not here and it'll only take five minutes.'

'Stop it right now!' And off went Mum looking very pink.

156.

Goodness knows what Kay had heard but I lifted up the stylus and apologised to her and said I had to go.

Frankie Vaughan was also a favourite of mine - especially with his recording of *Green Door* and also Lonnie Donegan, who made a series of hits: *Rock Island Line, Bring a little Water Sylvie, Don't you rock me Daddio, Putting on the style*, and *Cumberland Gap*. The Vipers were another skiffle group whose songs I liked, as well as Tommy Steele's *Rock with the caveman*.

My parents were still being strict about a television. We rented one for the school summer holidays in 1956 but it went back to the shop when we went back to school. I suppose what I did not have I did not miss.

That summer, I sat at the kitchen table with Dad's typewriter writing my first play. It was called *The First to Land* and was the story of a Viking invasion. I sat there thinking, then tapping the keys and alternately listening to the radio. If I was distracted from my typing it drove me mad when I made a mistake. There was no Tippex in those days and I was typing it on some of Dad's thin work paper - foolscap size. I still have the battered script of my Viking saga.

***

In the autumn of 1956 I moved up into the Upper Fifth. Now, the O Level GCE exams loomed. Unless one was very bright, seven subjects were the maximum number permitted to be taken in one exam period. I dropped Geography and Scripture and finally decided on English Grammar, English Literature, Biology, Maths, History, French and Art,

Being the hoarder and collector I fully admit to being, I still have the official GCE exam papers I took at the end of the Upper Fifth year in the Summer of 1957. These are interesting, not only for their existence, but also for some of the content, which in some subjects I could not attempt to answer now.

On some papers I ticked off the options I chose. Questions on Shakespeare's *Richard II*, Tennyson's selected poems and Jane Austen's *Northanger Abbey* were selected on the English Lit. paper. I remember greatly enjoying *Richard II* and the Tennyson poems, but was not so keen on *Northanger Abbey*.

I think I could still make a good try at The English Language paper, and to my delight, I can still manage a reasonable translation of the French into English paper but, Mathematics! Papers on Algebra and Arithmetic, each two hours long and Geometry of two and a half hours, just make my eyes roll now.

Also, I have forgotten most of the British and European History (1871-1939) I was taught, although I am sure it is 'up there somewhere'. In Biology, I do remember most of the subject matter. The only Art paper I have, shows where I happily ticked the theatre design question It required me to design costumes for four suggested characters from the Arabian Nights, in three hours.

Apart from Art we usually sat our exams in the gym and it was often hot weather so all the windows were open. In the silence of the exam room we could hear people chatting as they walked by. In difficult moments I used to think 'How can they be so cheerful out there while I'm sitting in here going through agonies?' or 'Why can't I be out there?' or simply 'It's not fair!' and then I would get on with the exam paper. Mercifully any Biology or Art practical exams were held in a laboratory or studio, where the temperature was more comfortable.

In the Summer term we entered some scenes from Shakespeare's *Taming of the Shrew* for the Drama Competition. I even have photographs of Kay as Katharina and myself as Petruchio, but we do not get a mention in the School magazine

Life changed as some of my friends left at the end of this term. The ones I best knew were going on to study medicine and nursing. They were Carole Fisher, with whom I washed my hair in rainwater, Liz Weller, whose family held the memorable children's Christmas parties in Southwell and Anne Yates, who also listened to Radio Luxembourg under the bedclothes.

Anne was famous for setting herself up as a fortune teller in the store room in the large Art studio. This was part of a school Bring and Buy sale in aid of the new playing field. The room was made quite dark with draped material and Anne was dressed like a gipsy and had a crystal ball on a small table. I cannot remember how much she charged, but there was a queue outside her door all afternoon. And all done by guess work. Or was it?

I passed my O Level subjects with B grades, in all but Mathematics, which I passed with Grade C. In 1957 C was average and B was above average. With a view to applying to the Central School of Speech and Drama I intended to take English, History and Art at A Level.

To my horror I was put in the Economics History set for A Level studies. I had little or no interest in the Economic element of History; I was not good at it and I was told that the other set was full. Enraged, I went into a state of fury, and asked my parents to complain.

My suspicion was that girls planning to go to University had first choice. My Mum was the last person to make a fuss whenever it came to official-dom and Dad only made a few platitudinous comments. As far as I know he did nothing. The message was that the school knew best and I should not cause trouble.

I felt inordinately frustrated and furious and could not sleep. In the end I complained to my class teacher and said that if I could not have my pre-ferred choice in History, I would please, like to take French instead.

Sometime later, in the middle of an art class, I was summoned to the headmistress's office. This was a highly unusual event and everybody stared at me as I left the room.

I suddenly felt very wobbly as I knocked on Miss Milford's door, and realised I might look scruffy in my art overall. Her office was a small, but elegant, high-ceilinged airy room, painted pale blue. It overlooked the play-ground through tall casement windows, all of which made me feel even scruffier and wobblier. The conversation went like this:

Miss M.: *Now Judith, I gather you have decided you would rather take French than History at Advanced level.*

Me: *Yes Miss Milford.*

Miss M: *Can you tell me why?*

Me: *Well, Miss Milford I have been put in the Economics set which I am not so interested in and am not very good at and I have been told the general History set is full, so I would prefer to change to French, please.*

Miss M. *I don't see why you should not be able to do that, Judith. You can change to French.*

Me: *Oh thank you, thank you very much Miss Milford.*

I stood rooted to the spot in a golden haze of incredulity, which quickly changed to joy and belief that Miss Milford had fixed it for me.

Miss M. *Off you go then.*

Me: *Oh thank you Miss Milford. Thank you very much.*

As I left the room the tall door closed with a gentle click and I stood at the bottom of the elegant staircase of Block A, almost unable to believe that I had been given what I had wished for

It was the first time I realised I could have some power over my future. I was fifteen years old and have never forgotten that moment. I was now even more determined to make my way to a speech and drama college in London.

26

Holiday Jobs

I had a variety of holiday jobs throughout my school years. When I was thirteen years old I worked in a local chemist shop, just down the hill in West Bridgford. It was run by a Mrs Evans and it was just the two of us. At first it was a Saturday job, but later, in a school holiday it was for a couple of weeks. In those days shops closed for one afternoon a week and very few were open on Sundays.

Mrs Evans was tall and thin; she had short curly grey hair, wore a long white overall, and round glasses. She peered through these at customers, also the shelves, when she was looking for something I could not find, and occasionally, me.

She first gave me a white overall to wear, which was far too large for me, but after a few days she found me a smaller one. There was a little back room with shelves full of all sizes and shapes of jars and boxes, and a gas ring at the end of some rubber tubing. In here, every morning, while I kept shop, Mrs Evans boiled a pan of milk on the gas ring to make our instant coffee.

She would lean over it, stirring away at the milk while humming, and smoking a cigarette with a long piece of ash that was always about to drop in the saucepan, but never did.

Mrs Evans seemed to know exactly when to flip it into the ash tray. Now I am writing about smoking, I should mention that my father always smoked and my mother did now and then. In fact, most adults smoked and so did quite a lot of children.

Mrs Evans was my first 'boss' and she was a bit sharp at times, but never grouchy. I do not think she could have had help in the shop before me, as at first she was very curt when she asked me to do something specific. She was like a sergeant, talking in short staccato phrases in a high pitched voice. At first she made me jump with, 'Judith! - wash the saucepan - and the mugs

- will you - please,' and, 'Where's the aspirin - have you moved it? - dear?' or, 'Hold the fort - Judith, I have to go to the lavatory'.

It was all good experience for me, I was soon able to get on with tasks that were part of our daily routine, so Mrs Evans did not have to keep asking me to do them. I learned a lot about shop life, that it could be very boring when there were no customers and frantic when there was a queue.

For a while I had to check the price of each item with Mrs Evans and she operated the till, but after a few days she trusted me to do everything. However, I had learnt to always ask her if I was not sure about anything.

Mrs Evans knew many of the customers by name, as most of them lived locally and came in frequently. There were some customers she did not let me serve. They asked for items I had not heard of.

Once a man came in and I asked if I could help him and he said he would like to talk to Mrs Evans who was serving another customer. Later, when we had a break, Mrs Evans said it was not that he did not think I could help him, it was because he was a bit shy. I asked her what Durex was and she said it was to stop people having babies. I asked her why people did not want to have babies. She looked at me through her glasses and said, 'Some people just don't want to have babies,' and then she got up and went into into the shop.

Mrs Evans was really a good soul and I remember her very fondly.

***

My friend Sheila's dad owned a greengrocer's not far from Mrs Evan's chemist shop, and I worked there for two school holidays. It was very different to the chemist shop, for a start the overalls were green. It was much harder work, and could also be very cold, as the door was always open and sometimes we had to go outside to serve items displayed in boxes in front of the shop.

There were two other women assistants who worked there and they were really good fun. We laughed a lot about funny shaped vegetables and one of them was a bit naughty as she sometimes made fun of a customer, especially if one was being difficult. When we were rushed off our feet and the phone rang she would answer it gloomily, 'Wilford Crematorium.'

It was probably a customer wanting to make an order, but whoever it was they always rang off. The first time I heard her do it I could not believe what she was doing, especially as she gave me a huge wink.

I loved going into the flower room at the back of the shop. The scent of fresh flowers was overwhelming and I was fascinated by the way the florist made up the bouquets and wreaths. We always took time with customers who came in to order flowers. Often it was for a happy occasion, like a birthday or anniversary, but it could as often be for a funeral.

Early on I was struggling with a woman who had had a bereavement, she was clearly very upset and could not decide what to have written on the card. I would write something on the docket, then she would change her mind and I had to tear out the docket and start again.

This happened several times, but at last she seemed happy with what we agreed. I must have spent at least half an hour with her. In the back room when we had a coffee break one of the girls gave me useful advice on making suggestions for funeral cards.

'What you do,' she said, ' is when you have all the information about the funeral director and where and when the funeral is and what sort of flowers or wreath they would like, if by then, they haven't already told you whether it was a close relation or not and they can't make up their minds what to say on the card, most of them really appreciate it if you can suggest something. For example you can suggest, 'In Loving Memory,' if it's for someone close, or, 'With Deepest Sympathy,' if not so close. Then on the docket you write either ILM or WDS and add additional comments and names as required.'

It seemed a bit callous to me, but I never let the customer see the abbreviations I was using and it saved a fair amount of time. Also, most people appreciated the suggestion of some kind of formal phrase.

In that job, one of my fears was that I would discover a deadly spider amongst the bananas. They (that's the bananas) arrived in long wooden boxes with Fyffes stamped on the side, and they had to be levered open by one of the men on the staff. We all stood back a pace or two when the lid first creaked upwards, but nothing ever jumped out at us.

I liked working at Sheila's dad's shop but it was good to get home. All I

163.

wanted to do was have a wash and rid myself of any fruit or vegetable stains I had acquired during the day.

***

Sometime later I had a holiday job in the Co-op greengrocer's in town. I was glad I had previously worked in a similar shop and was soon used to the routine. Customers in town were often in a hurry and we never had to take any long orders on the telephone. I was there a couple of weeks and I worked with a brilliant little dark-haired woman who was never still and always had something to say that made me laugh.

One day we had a glut of mushrooms which we were selling very cheaply. Word must have got around to the nearby offices and shops as we sold them continually, until closing time. As the boxes emptied my colleague would dash off to the back room store and return with another one.

She kept saying, 'Oh this is a funny day? Don't you think we're having a funny day?' and then she would ask her customer if he or she was having a funny day. We became almost hysterical. As we closed for the next day we both noticed our hands were stained dark brown from handling so many mushrooms.

'Oh dear,' she said, 'That's funny - I told you we were having a funny day.'

I said, 'Well you said we were having a funny day,' and we went our separate ways home.

Later that evening Mum asked me if I had had a good day and I said 'Well, it was a funny day really,' and hooted with laughter. I tried to explain and my dear Mum laughed feebly; she clearly had no idea what was so funny. It was a while before the mushroom stains came out.

***

When I finished my O level exams I got my first waitressing job. It was in a large department store on the Old Market Square, called Griffin and Spalding. It was a smart establishment with two restaurants. One was large, where they served lunches and high teas, and the other was smaller and was called The Cona Bar.

My first job was as a waitress in the main restaurant. I had never done the job before and was thrown in at the deep end. We wore green nylon overalls and the first thing we had to do in the morning was lay up our tables.

First the table cloths, also green, went on the tables, then the serviettes and bread plates and cutlery, then finally the cruet which included English mustard and we had to mix it freshly every morning; a task that always made my eyes run.

Most of this tableware was in the huge kitchen and had to be carried out and across the restaurant to where our tables were. Each waitress had a 'station' which was a small cupboard and drawers where spare cutlery was kept and there was also a chair which we never had time to sit on.

We each had several tables to serve, but the permanent more experienced women were keen to keep as many customers as possible as they needed the tips. I must have had five or six tables to wait on, but I never felt that the other waitresses resented my being there.

Once I was used to the system it was quite a fun job, but very hard work. I was amazed at the size of the kitchen and all the shiny stainless steel surfaces. There was a giant of a man who worked there called Bill. He was a deaf mute who 'manned' the washing up machine. This was a huge curved metal cover which straddled two big sinks. Soiled crockery and cutlery was placed on wide wire trays, over which Bill sprinkled detergent. One at a time these were slid over the first sink and Bill slapped a lever over and down to the left and the metal cover rolled over the soiled tableware.

Then Bill pressed a button and there was a rumbling and splashing sound for a few minutes. He pressed another button and there was a different kind of watery whooshing sound. Sometime later he lifted up the right side of the cover and pulled the tray out with the clean crockery and cutlery steaming and glistening. That load would be pushed further along the shiny work surface to dry and the whole process started again.

Bill was very protective of his machine and was upset if anyone tried to interfere with it. One of the waitresses was desperate to have some clean cutlery and she lifted the cover before the rinsing time was completely finished. Water shot out all over the place. Poor Bill was mortified and waved his arms around making terrifying incoherent moans.

The Manager, Mr Carruthers, a tall thin military looking man with a moustache, who always wore a suit, was summoned from his office to calm Bill down. This he did, asking Bill to look him in the eye and reassuring him that it was not his fault and he would not lose his job. Well, whether or not Bill understood what he was saying, Mr Carruthers was to be admired, because Bill stopped making weird noises and waving his arms and was back to normal after being given a cup of tea.

Lunchtime could be very busy, especially on Wednesdays, which was market day, when the restaurant was packed. We closed briefly between lunch and teatime, but before we could take our lunch break we had to clear away and lay up for teas before we left for the staff room.

One market day I served two young lads who were slightly late coming in for lunch and they had the full three courses which they quickly consumed and signalled to me to go over. I assumed they wanted the bill.

'That were brilliant,' one of them said.

'Grand!' said the other.

'Oh the dessert?' I said, 'Yes they are rather nice.'

'We'll have it again,' one of them said.

'Oh good,' I said, ' Two more desserts?'

'No, we'll have the whole lot again' they said.

'All three courses?' I squeaked.

'Yep.' 'Yep,' they nodded, grinning.

By the time they left, the restaurant was empty except for me. I whizzed around clearing their table and relaying it. I was just in time, as Mr Carruthers opened the door for teatime customers.

As I washed out the mustard pots in the kitchen I cried with frustration as well as the fumes, but the lads had been very nice and gave me a really good tip. The girls said they would cover my tables while I took a break. I gave myself ten minutes to sit down in the staff room, and then I was back out there again.

Unfortunately, the heat and rushing and general stress affected me and I came out in an awful rash on my neck. My infant eczema had returned and nothing seemed to cure it until I went back to school.

My day to day contact with the waitresses taught me a lot about how other people lived their lives. Most of them were good natured and friendly and several had children.

The conversations in the small staff room could be very coarse and sometimes puzzling to someone like me with my cosy suburban upbringing. After a couple of weeks I had worked out that at least three of them were part time prostitutes and one of them was very badly treated by her pimp.

She was short and overweight and had the saddest laugh I ever heard; it was like a high pitched machine gun with a sigh at the end. Another woman who was tall and ruddy complexioned was Irish and a devout Catholic. I had a discussion with her about the gold in Catholic churches and asked her why it wasn't used to help the poor.

She looked shocked and said, 'But tis for the Glory of God,' and that was it. She was the one who talked at length about the fun of wearing a long nightie when going to bed with someone as they had to, 'fight to get at me.'

None of them had any money to spare, but if someone was having a really bad day they would share their tips. Well, some of them did.

One day Mr Carruthers called me into his office. He always stood upright and walked as though he might have been in the army. I suppose he was quite good looking with his grey hair and moustache. He was always well mannered and polite, to customers and staff alike.

He asked me if I was any good at maths. I replied that I was all right at it. He then gave me the task of checking over his account totals. At first I found this interesting, but after an hour it bored me to tears. The girls made some ribald comments and had a good laugh at me when I returned to the staff room on the next break. I was not completely stupid about possible advances from men, but I did not think Mr Carruthers had any dubious intentions. Anyway, I much preferred the hum drum rush of the restaurant to sitting in a quiet office on my own.

The next time I applied for work in the restaurant I was put on the Cona Bar. This was supervised by a pleasant little woman, Mrs Simpson, and I was to be her assistant supervisor. We both wore lilac coloured nylon overalls. She was a quiet person and always looked pale but at that time in my life I was not very aware of other people's possible problems.

I was glad not to be rushing around so much but I did have more responsibility. Soon, Mrs Simpson trusted me to work a few hours on my own and then even whole days. Looking back now I wonder if she was unwell. In the end she was off for a week on holiday and she returned looking really healthy. Perhaps she just needed a rest.

The Cona bar was a much smaller restaurant with a simpler menu. It was more like a cafe which served toasted snacks and delicious desserts. The waitresses had to go into the kitchen to order cold items like salads, sandwiches and ice cream concoctions. It was here, if we had a rush on, that I became a whizz at making Banana Splits, Cream Chantillys and Coupe Jacques.

There was a counter at the side of the Cona Bar, where all the hot drinks were served. Two or three shiny metal urns boiled water, heated milk and percolated coffee. The counter was also stacked with trays of cups and saucers and on the wall behind there were shelves of teapots and jugs.

One of the kitchen staff operated this counter and the waitresses would put in their orders for teas and coffees. Beside this beverage counter there was a square hatch in the wall where the waitresses stuck their dockets for grilled snacks on to a spike.

The kitchen area on the other side of this hatch was ruled by another deaf mute who cooked all the grills and toasted sandwiches. Her name was Mavis and she always had a very red face, no doubt due to the heat from the grill.

She was incredibly hard working and efficient, but waitresses had to write their order very clearly on the docket. If Mavis pushed an incorrect grill through the hatch and the waitress complained, Mavis would explode with fury and point to the now very crumpled docket, attempting to enunciate: 'You wrote....whatever she had cooked' If the waitress disagreed, Mavis looked as though she might explode again.

That was when Mrs Simpson or I was called to intervene and dear Mavis eventually calmed down, muttering in her own way as she cooked the correct dish.

168.

Thankfully this only happened once or twice when I was on duty. There was a close to disastrous start to one of my first mornings on my own. The floor staff all clocked in at about 8.30 - 9am, laid up their tables and had time to have a quick break before the customers started arriving around 10am.

Before the day really began, Mrs Simpson and I would have a 'little sit down' at a table near the tea and coffee urns. She usually had a small pot of tea and I had what was then known as Russian tea in a glass in a metal holder. This is now usually known as lemon tea, but I felt frightfully swish sitting there as a supervisor toying with my Russian tea.

This particular morning there was a problem. As I said, I was on my own; the Cona bar looked ready to go and when I asked Cynthia, the girl on the teas and coffee counter, for my Russian tea, she alerted me to the fact that the containers were taking ages to heat up. In fact, they were stone cold. It was about a quarter to ten and they took a while to achieve the required temperature.

Cynthia did not inspire confidence; she did not wear her white overall well and had a fuzz of fair hair which squashed out around her white hat. Her round spectacles emphasised her vacant look and she had a manner of speech which could never indicate a state of urgency. She peered constantly at the cold urns in turn as though willing them to heat up. In desperation I asked her if she had turned on the mains electricity.

She turned to look at the switch, then turned back to me, a finger on the bottom lip of her open mouth and said, 'Oh, no. I forgot. Thank you, Judy'.

We were ready in time for the first orders for coffee; thankfully the coffee percolator heated up more quickly than the hot water for tea. The odd thing was that when Cynthia started serving coffees and teas for the waitresses to collect, she was surprisingly organised and fast on her feet.

In one of my morning conversations with Mrs Simpson, I mentioned that I was surprised how many handicapped staff worked in the catering department. There was also another woman, a general help in the kitchen, who always looked lost.

Mrs Simpson explained to me that all large stores were obliged to employ a certain number of handicapped people. In our store the practice was to place them in the catering department where most of the time they were out of sight of the general public. I was shocked.

In the Cona Bar the customers were usually on the move. Most of those who came in early wanted a quick cup of coffee and maybe a brief chat with a friend and then they were off again.

Later in the morning, women with shopping bags with fashion labels on them arrived and they could take ages to settle at a table. They stood by the entrance desk, as they removed their gloves, looking round to see if there was anyone there that they knew.

Their thoughtless habit was to carelessly drop their bags down where waitresses or customers could easily trip over them. It was one of my responsibilities to check there were no hazards between the tables. If they met friends there would be a great deal of pulling items out of bags and chattering about their purchases. They might stay on for lunch, which, as the menu was simple, was much quicker to serve than in the other restaurant. The staff also usually had a break before the afternoon teas.

One afternoon a group of young men and women came in. They were lively and laughed a lot. After tea and cakes they paid and left apart from one young man. He poured himself another cup of tea and then leaned over to the centre of the table to the sugar bowl, to pick up a cube of sugar with the sugar tongs.

He just could not do it. It took ages for him to pick one up and however careful he was, he either dropped the sugar lump back in the bowl or carried it half way to his cup before dropping it on the cloth. You could see him sigh and start again. It was one of the funniest things I had ever seen. One of the waitresses whispered in my ear, "Ee 's pissed. Absolutely sozzled.' Amazingly, later, he managed to pay his bill and totter out of the restaurant, much to my relief. That was another time when Mrs Simpson happened to be absent.

Despite these challenging events, I never felt insecure or worried about dealing with them. I knew I could summon up some kind of back up, the cashier would have rung straight through to some security office if things had really got out of hand.

And Mr Carruthers was only a minute away. AND the waitresses were a pretty feisty crowd.

***

I can't remember how much I earned in my previous holiday jobs, but I do remember that working on Christmas postal deliveries was one of the best paid you could get for the number of days and hours worked.

I was lucky enough to work for the post office for two Christmases in a row. Usually the work was available for a week before Christmas and we went right through to Boxing day, which we had off.

It was hard getting up very early on dark, cold, usually foggy and often icy mornings, but it was only for a few days. There was a delivery on Christmas day, which was great fun as everyone was in such a good mood both in the sorting office and out in the street.

My very first day, when I signed on at the main sorting office, was as though I had been transported into a different world from the dark cold one outside. I was drawn in to a huge, brightly-lit, warm warehouse, with rows and rows of long work surfaces backed by shelves of pigeon holes large enough to take a wedge of letters.

This was the sorting office. The pigeon holes were labelled with names of streets and if they were very long streets, there could be two or three pigeon holes for one street. Post codes had not been introduced and the postmen stood sorting piles of letters by the numbers on their addresses into the pigeon holes on their rounds.

There was a very busy atmosphere with the postmen shouting jolly comments to each other. Christmas was approaching and the arrival of temporary assistant teenage helpers to ease their seasonal overload must have brightened their day.

I was introduced to my postman, who was a very nice man called Frank. He showed me how to sort the letters into streets and then numbers. As he had been there well before I arrived, the sorting was soon finished and we tied the letters into street bundles. We then divided all the mail into two bags, with the bundles in order of delivery. He slung one bag over his shoulder and I did the same, it was pretty heavy and he said:

'Right, breakfast!' and we set off through the cold early morning streets to a cafe, which was warm, noisy and smoky inside. I had my first ever bacon and egg sandwich and it was one of the most delicious things I had ever tasted. With a mug of hot tea, it was just the best start to a postal round.

We then caught a bus a short way to an area north of the Old Market Square with which I was not familiar. I kept my eyes open to remember the route and where we got off the bus.

We walked a little way and then started on the round. The idea was that we would split the round and take half each, but he showed me the ropes for the whole round; where some front doors were tucked round the side of the building; where half hidden letter boxes were; where to watch out for a dog if it had been let out and others where the dog barked like mad behind the door and snatched the letters out of your hand as you pushed them through the letterbox.

There were a couple of houses where they liked you to knock or ring the bell when you put the mail through the letterbox and others where the owner might whip the door open when you arrived. Frank told me I must walk away once I had handed them their mail. Otherwise I could get drawn into a long conversation about a particular letter they were expecting and you could be there for hours.

He was quite funny sometimes and very helpful, but my head was buzzing with so much information. I hardly noticed my bag becoming lighter, but suddenly both Frank's and mine were empty, the round was over and we caught the bus back to town. The following days I was on my own and responsible for delivering a morning and afternoon round. After the second delivery I went straight home having left my bag at the sorting office.

Our Christmas day round was comparatively lighter than the previous days. It felt really good to be out in the streets and seeing all the Christmas lights on in people's houses. It was probably my imagination, but it felt as though there was 'something' in the air. People wished me 'Happy Christmas,' and I was given the odd tip, and they were often given by people from whom I least expected them. However I did not hang around the doors

172.

with the barking dogs.

The next Christmas was similar, except I had a different postman and a different round. The only memorable thing was the weather; it was a freezing and foggy December. My boyfriend Martin was also doing postal work and gave me a lift in on his motorbike.

One icy, foggy dark morning I was waiting for him by my Dad's garage and I heard a motorbike coming slowly up the hill, and turning left to where I was waiting. There was a scraping sound of metal on road and the engine sound stopped. In the following silence I could hear running footsteps coming towards me. Martin stumbled out of the fog.

'Are you OK?" I asked.

'Yes – I think I am,' was the panted reply.

'How's the bike?'

'I don't know.'

He explained that he had skidded on an icy patch, felt the bike sliding away under him, let go, and managed to jump over the handle bars. He had continued running forward, partly propelled by the pace of the bike and also to avoid being tripped up by the sliding bike.

We walked to the corner and found the bike lying on its side. Everything seemed to be working, including the lights which were essential that morning. So we set off up town, driving very slowly.

27

Lower 6
September 1957- September 1958

The last two years of my school life were such a busy jumble of socialising and hard work that apart from a few dates, it is difficult to keep to a chronicle of events. At least the school timetable was simpler. Three subjects: English, French and Art, each covering a broad area of study, some to be learned by heart. We also had a games afternoon each week.

Feeling exuberant since my transfer to French, I accosted the course teacher, Miss Hollyer, on the staircase in A block. Our conversation went like this:

'Good morning Miss Hollyer. I'm coming to your French Class.'

Miss Hollyer looked at me with piercing eyes.

'Are you sure? It's the Advanced level Course.'

'Yes,' I said, suppressing a creeping feeling of deflation,

'I've transferred from History'.

'Oh I see ' she said ' Well then, see you in class.'

'Yes, thank you,' I said. Clearly Miss Hollyer had not been informed of this upstart joining her class. I knew I was going to find the translations tough, but I loved the language and had passed O level French with a B Grade, which was above average. I resolved to impress her.

Miss Gornall and Miss Dodwell continued to teach us English and Miss Hyde a new teacher, taught us Art. There were only seven of us in the A Level class, and Kay was one of them. She was far more skilled than I was at drawing and I especially remember admiring a painting of hers which was an abstract interpretation of electricity pylons in a landscape. However I could hold my own with theatre designs of costumes and sets.

It was about this time we had been asked to design a school Christmas card. We worked on scraper board which was a black surfaced card with a layer of white china clay sandwiched between the black surface and card beneath. To make the picture you used small sharp tools to etch into the white clay below. If you made a mistake it was not too difficult to paint over it in black Indian Ink to match the black surface.

Over the next two Christmases three of my designs were chosen to be printed. One of them was of the main gate to the school and the large houses behind it, which looked rather spooky in black and the other two were caricatures of our school symbol, an owl.

One of these was a large owl, with a tiny owl sitting on a frosty branch of a tree by moonlight. The other one, which they printed in red, was an owl in mortar board and gown with a lantern and snow lightly falling. I was so thrilled to see them in print.

This thrill was slightly dulled by my hearing a conversation between Kay and Miss Hyde. Kay was disappointed her design was not chosen. I heard Miss Hyde saying, 'Well yes, I know, but you see, this is what they want,' shaking her head and indicating one of my owl cards. I realised Miss Hyde could have been trying to comfort Kay, but she should have made sure no one else was within earshot, particularly me. I got over it quickly enough thinking, 'Well if that's what they want, aren't I lucky?

Kay was one of the prettiest girls I knew at school. She had dark wavy hair and eyes that sparkled. She was especially popular when we were lower down the school and other girls used to scuffle to sit next to her with shouts like 'My turn' and 'Bags I sit next to Kay next lesson then!'

I am not sure what happened to her after we left school and I had gone to London. All I do know is that she went to Nottingham College of Art and after that to Hornsey Art College.

Apart from that little blip with Miss Hyde, I loved the art classes. As well as theatre design I remember painting, composition and still life. But I was frustrated by my ineptness at life drawing and portraiture. Even so I spent some of my happiest times at school in the art rooms.

One hot summer's afternoon, Kay and I were working away on our own. We knew Miss Hyde was in the staff room if we needed any help. It was well after school finishing time but we carried on.

Miss Hyde suddenly appeared with a plate of curled up cucumber sandwiches from the staff room tea. Despite their dried up condition Kay and I wolfed them down.

***

I was becoming more aware of myself as 'growing up'. My hair was much longer and I had a pony tail with a long fringe. The fringe was partly to hide my spotty forehead, although at one point my mother suggested it was making the spots worse. They did eventually go, but not before I tried using 'Crème Puff' to cover them. 'Crème Puff' was a compressed powder face make up. When I went dancing I used a very pale pink lipstick, which was 'in' and I also tried some black eyeliner and mascara.

This came in a small case containing a tiny brush and block of black mascara. The block had to be moistened with water (we all used spit) and the brush scrubbed lightly across it so some mascara was picked up and used to enhance our eyelashes. I also experimented with false eyelashes which were fiddly to put on, but could look pretty convincing. A friend of mine was at a dance when her false eyelashes fell off. Her boyfriend thought she had insects crawling over her jumper.

It must have been about this time that Zoe Newton was the Pinta Milka girl and she had streaks of blonde in her fringe. At school one day, two or three of us who had fringes, went into the chemistry lab to filch some hydrogen peroxide (bleach). We must have come out looking like badgers. When my mum saw it she said firmly but kindly 'I think, that's enough, Judy,' and I did not carry on with it because I had discovered 'Light and Bright' which was the 'in' hair lightening treatment and much kinder to hair.

One of the troubles with having long hair was split ends, and to combat that there was a product called 'Vitapointe,' a very oily cream. You only needed to use the tiniest amount on the split ends or your hair could go greasy overnight. Shampooing and drying it was a major event. Cosmetics were banned at school, but some girls got away with it by using them very subtly.

Socially my life was slowly looking up. I continued to go to the Saturday afternoon dance classes at Burnside hall. Friends had parties and as we were now in the 6th form, we could go to the Inter 6th dance classes held for the boys and girls in the 6th form at the two high schools.

My father was as strict as ever and I always had to be home by 10.30pm wherever I was going. I had to ask him for a 'late pass' when I was going to one of Kay's parties, as she lived out of town in Chilwell. He said no, with no offer of giving me a left there or back. In the end I was given a lift home by a friend's father and I was nearly half an hour late. Dad was waiting for me in the hall and was furious:

'How dare you come home this late at night when I specifically told you to be home by 10.30? '

He refused to listen to my excuses and said, 'You should be here to help your mother.'

To which I answered, 'why can't Michael help?'

To my surprise, this stalled him for a second, so I stamped up the stairs muttering, 'It's not fair.'

Looking back now, I can see that my general behaviour had become that of a typical 'teenager.' Bill Haley introduced this term on his first tour of Britain in early 1957. Until then, all young people had been called 'adolescents.'

But with my Dad, it was not just the curfew. It was all mixed up with other feelings including a deep disappointment which I did not recognise until later on in life. I had always expected, at least, hoped, that my dad and I would do things together and he would even take me places on my own sometimes, just me, no brothers.

I do not really know what I had in mind, but whatever it was, he never did it. Yes, he did take me to the flying club now and then, but I did not feel that was enough and furiously wrote about it in my diary.

Each year I bought a big Boots diary and in it wrote copious accounts of the injustices of the world. When I left home to go to college I ripped them up and threw them in the rubbish.

Dad stuck to his 10.30 curfew and, as the latest bus to get me home on time left the Old Market Square at ten minutes past ten, I missed the ending of several films, including Bonjour Tristesse, which I did not catch up with for several years.

177.

Apart from the odd kiss or hug at Burnside hall, my one date so far had been going to a film with Graham, one of the boys I regularly met in the fields. We sat near the back and held hands with our heads close together. He had so much Brylcreem on his hair that one side of my face and hair was all greasy when we came out of the cinema. I was home before my 10.30 curfew. Graham didn't ask me out again. When we met up a few years later he said, ' You were so quiet,' which I thought must have been a fob off as it is a bit tricky to be loud in a cinema.

There was one other boy I really liked. I cannot remember how we met, but he was tall and thin and had a racing bike When he went to the Isle of Wight for a holiday he sent me two postcards. I thought he was going off me because the second one had fewer words than the first. We never went out together, just talked and talked when we met.

There was also another boy who used to sit outside our house on his bike. I would be upstairs in my room doing my homework and when I looked out of the window he would be there. I knew who he was and we always said hello when we met, but not much more.

My mother mentioned him to me and I said, 'Oh yes I know, he's often there,' and she said, laughing, 'You ought to get friendly with him. He comes from a very rich family you know.' I did not know, but it made no difference to how I felt about him. I did not think it was creepy, he was just a bit of a nuisance. I suppose these days he might be called a stalker.

Then, at the Inter 6th dancing classes I got to know a boy who I saw on the bus to school. He was called Martin and was very pale. We had things in common; he went to the Scouts and church, liked hiking, was hoping to go to university in London and he could be very funny.

He sometimes met me from Guides which I thought was really nice of him. We walked back to my home having a bit of a cuddle on the way. One of his friends, Roger was going out with my friend, Carol and sometimes we all went out together.

As I got to know Martin better I realised he was not very healthy as he used an inhaler for asthma and he had an digestive problem called colitis. But generally they did not affect him too badly. He lived down the hill, only ten minutes walk away.

My parents met him and thought he was 'all right'. I was asked to tea at his place to meet his mum and dad, his younger sister Jean and even younger brother Peter. His mother had laid on a scrumptious tea, with home made ginger biscuits, cake and sandwiches.

We all sat at a table in the back room being very polite to each other. Peter, who was quite young, suddenly piped up, 'What's that for?' pointing at the slop bowl on the table, which matched the cups and saucers. Martin's mother giggled and said it was for tipping the tea leaves into from a used cup.

Peter's face was a picture of screwed up disgust and everyone at the table burst out laughing, Martin's mother too. Teabags were not so popular in 1958. Generally, tea was brewed in a pot with loose tea leaves and boiling water. A few tea leaves usually escaped down the spout from the pot into each cup of tea, where they sank to the bottom.

People said you could read a person's fortune from the tea leaves left in someone's cup. However, if there was a slop bowl on the table those tea leaves would be tipped in. A slop basin was considered rather posh and most families did not bother with one. Hence the hilarity as Martin's mother tried to impress. From that teatime I came to know the family very well and Martin and I often spent an evening there and very few at my home.

It was about this time when rather than catching the trolley bus up to school, Martin and I used to join some other friends in the Old Market Square and walk to our schools, the boys splitting off once we came to the Arboretum.

This was the time of, 'Did you listen to the Goons last night?' or, 'Did you listen to Pooh last night?' These two programmes: *The Goons* and *Winnie the Pooh* became cult listening. We imitated the different characters and became helpless with laughter as we walked.

We also discussed the subjects we were taking at A Level and why and what college we hoped we might go to; who got caught wearing makeup and who was told off for not having a school badge showing. It was a happy uncomplicated time and good to be with friends.

179.

My life was full, I continued to go swimming each week and became interested in a lifesaving class. I had earlier learned the life saving technique in the Guides, as well as at school. It was called Artificial Respiration. First the patient's throat was checked for the removal of any constriction; he/she was rolled over into the prone position, the head to one side and the arms and hands, palms down, placed on the floor in line with the head. The patient was given a number of chest compressions to (hopefully) get their lungs and heart going again. This preceded the Kiss of Life technique, now the preferred method of resuscitation

This lifesaving course was organised by the school and one evening a week I went with some friends to a swimming pool further along the Mansfield Road. We had an hour of learning life saving techniques in the water. We were often divided into pairs when one of us was the panicking drowning person and the other was the rescuer.

It was really hard work, but a great thing to do to rid our heads of the tension of working for exams. The course was held when the evenings were cold, dark and wintry and it was so lovely to walk into the warm, chlorinated atmosphere of the pool, but not so good queuing for the bus to go home again. I passed the test and received a certificate.

The School play that year was a double bill, Sophocles' *Electra* and Christopher Fry's *The Boy with a Cart*. Carol took the lead part of Electra and Kay played her sister Chrysothemis. I was a member of the Chorus whose role was to sympathise with Electra in her grief and to emphasise the drama as each tragic event unfolded.

This was not a good experience for me. I was going through a bad fainting phase, hormones maybe, or my undiagnosed low blood pressure. In one performance I ended up tottering off stage to collapse through the curtains at the side.

Miss Gornall gave us a pep talk before the last show, which I knew was aimed at me. I didn't blame her at all and I got through it, but came off stage in an absolute pool of sweat, thinking, 'How on earth am I going to cope at drama school?'

28.

First Aid, Walking & a Motorbike

It was becoming urgent for me to decide which college to apply to, so I sent off for some brochures. I really wanted to go to London, but I wrote to all of them around the country and received a confusing array to choose from.

My parents' concerns for my financial security in my future life manifested themselves in different ways. Dad told me that he thought the theatrical world was, 'full of a lot of pimps and natter jacks.'

I was shocked by his view of theatrical people, considering what my mother was doing for a living when they met!

As an alternative, he suggested I joined the Women's Auxiliary Air Force. He tempted me with a publicity sheet about the WAAF, showing a group of women sailing and swimming off somewhere like Malta.

My mother said, 'I think it would be a good idea, dear, if you had a piece of paper, like a teaching certificate'.

So that, for better or worse, was where I compromised. I checked out some of the brochures and focussed on those in London that offered teaching qualifications. I also concentrated on seeing as much theatre and film as I could and developing my skills in speech and drama.

Highlights were seeing Laurence Olivier in the films of *Richard III and Henry V*, which I saw in a small cinema, just the other side of Trent Bridge. I went to matinées and each time sat in an almost empty auditorium where I was transported by the whole experience.

Another film that made a deep impression on me was *The Great Adventure*, a black and white Swedish film. It was not remarkable from the acting point of view, but the visual language of wild life, the changing seasons, and the voiced over narrative all melded together, and the result was stunning. I learned a great deal from this film, especially how the pace

181.

and beauty of visuals alone can tell a story.

I read many theatrical biographies, including Laurence Olivier's, of course.

While developing my speech and drama skills, I found a new teacher who lived in a flat in the buildings around the Midland Station. It was an amazing flat with tall windows and a comfortable jumble of elegant and practical furniture. I cannot recall my teacher's name, but she must have once been an actress, as she had that timbre of voice that indicates its past use in more heavily dramatic situations.

I have a misty picture of her in my mind; a slightly built, elderly woman who usually wore something black and long, with some lace somewhere. She had grey blonde hair and a pale pixie like face, with dark eyes which sometimes closed as she listened to me emoting. She had small but very expressive hands. I liked her a lot and was always slightly in awe of her.

In the April of 1958 I passed the Guildhall School of Music and Drama, Grade 4 Speech and Drama Exam and started preparing for Grade 5. So I felt I was doing all I could to persuade one of those colleges that I had a certain amount of ability and masses of enthusiasm.

My dear mum was also building up her own pile of certificates. Before she was married, when there was a real fear of a second world war, she trained for and gained, two Red Cross certificates, one for a course in First Aid and the second for Home Nursing.

Mercifully, Mum was never called upon to use these skills. World War II was over, but now hanging over us was the 'cold war' with Russia. I was generally ignorant of World affairs, but everyone was fully aware of the horrors of the atom bomb and the threat of its aftermath.

In early 1957 Mum attended a course with the St. John Ambulance Association, this time in First Aid to the Injured. She joined the Civil Defence Corps, Nottinghamshire Division in February 1958, to be ready to help in the event of an atomic disaster. She had a uniform and a tin helmet, and went to a Civil Defence evening once a week. Maybe she had a heightened sense of survival as she was expecting another baby.

I found Martin's reaction to the news of a new baby rather odd. I had always thought of the birth of a baby as being a happy event, but when I told him, he was rather negative and came out with comments about how it might affect us.

I did not know what to say. Maybe he thought my father's curfew would be moved earlier. He was quite a domineering and possessive boyfriend, behaviour which could become a nuisance. We had good times together, but if we had a row he would stride away from me and expect me to keep up with him.

Sometimes I did, but often I did not because I was fed up with him. So he could be walking several yards ahead of me while I walked behind, studiously keeping the same distance between us. Goodness knows what the neighbours thought.

***

Peter was born in June 1958 and he was a lovely baby. Because obstetrics had moved on so much, his birth was the first one for which Mum was conscious. That meant a lot to her, especially as she was an older mother. It must have been really hard for her at forty seven. I did not realise how hard until I had my own family.

Peter was a fractious baby at night and my father took to sleeping down-stairs in his office. Mum must have been exhausted for months. She had the rest of us and Big Granny to keep an eye on. Obviously I helped when I could. However my parents did get some help, I believe it was the Home Help service again.

I started going to evening service at the Methodist church in West Bridgford that Martin went to as his mother was a Methodist. She worked in the local library and cycled there every day. I liked her very much. I also liked the Methodist style of service. Compared to the Church of England it was much more lively. Everyone sang the hymns more lustily and the sermons had more relevance to the modern world. I heard Donald Soper speak, a famous socialist and pacifist. He was a handsome man with presence and an amazing voice.

I carried on going to the Guides in Edwalton, as did Sheila, my friend down the road. Together we had been planning for weeks to go on a Youth

Hostelling trip in the summer holidays. We had already been on several short Youth Hostel breaks with the Guides and were both good at looking after ourselves in open country.

The Lake District was our dream destination, so first we booked coach tickets from Nottingham to Keswick, returning from Kendal a week later. Then, perusing Ordnance Survey maps, we planned a walking route which we thought was doable and booked Youth Hostel accommodation along the way. The exact route and names of all the hostels escape me now, but we had a fantastic time.

After our first night in Keswick we set off on a damp morning. Once clear of the town we were confronted by a very steep hill. We needed to be sure that we were on the right track, as that first day was quite a long walk, and we were wary of making a time wasting mistake.

I asked a local if we were on the right track. He looked at us both and said, 'Are you going up there?' pointing up the hill.

We said yes we were and he said, 'You take care now, the mist can come down very fast up there.' I had a pang of 'Oh no, maybe we've bitten off more than we can chew,' but we thanked him and set off up the steep path.

It was a killing climb, possibly the hardest of the week, but once we were at the top we turned to look at the view and it was stunning. The town of Keswick was way down below and as I raised my eyes, the incredible landscape of the Lake District stretched as far as I could see.

The rest of the walking that day was mainly on the flat, which was just as well as our legs were aching from the climb. It rained a little and we were glad to get to the youth hostel where there was the usual warm drying room. Most hostels had one, often it was the boiler room that was set aside for hanging up wet clothes and drying out socks and walking boots.

One of the best things on these trips was meeting other people and swapping stories about routes and other hostels. Back then youth hostels were for walkers, no cars and no cyclists.

It was likely one might be sleeping in a bunk bed in a dormitory, and although some hostels provided supper and breakfast, often they did not; so a certain amount of self catering was necessary. The hostels varied

184.

greatly, from mansions to cottages. We stayed in a small one in the Duddon valley, where there was no warden. We had to cook our own meals and little things were jumping about on the soft furnishing.

Mercifully, the beds were clean, but we were glad to leave the next day. It was the only hostel that did not live up to expectations but it was a good story to tell afterwards, but not to our parents.

We met some great people on our travels, some were walking the same way, so we walked together. There was an American boy who joined us for a couple of days. He was good company and of great interest to me, a relation of Sam Wanamaker, the internationally known actor and producer who initiated the project to rebuild Shakespeare's Globe Theatre on the South Bank in London.

We had an amazing week and Sheila was great company. Since then I have held the Lake District close to my heart. Even now, I can see in my mind's eye, memories of views and walks which will stay with me forever.

The rest of that summer I worked at Griffin and Spalding. Martin acquired a motorbike, a BSA 250 and we spent several weekends stripping it down and replacing gaskets with thick brown paper. I was given a black crash helmet and he passed his test, so we could go out for a spin, which we literally did one afternoon after skidding on a gritty corner on a quiet country road.

The bike ended up on its side and slid underneath us. I was wearing a thick duffel jacket and the toggles were torn off it. My knee was bruised and Martin had grazed his leg quite badly. However, the bike was fine and we wobbled slowly back to West Bridgford. We agreed we would not tell our parents, fearful of accusations of going too fast, and not being experienced enough for a pillion passenger etc...

I hid my duffel jacket in the little cloakroom under the stairs and spent the evening at home, feeling decidedly peculiar and cold. I recognised this as shock, so drank several cups of hot sweet tea. I went to bed early, making the excuse that I was going to revise. I lay down, and suddenly started crying. I put my head under the covers and my mother came into my room saying 'Judy, are you all right?'

185.

'Smf, yes thanks.' I snuffled.

'Martin's father has just rung and said that you and Martin fell off the bike.'

'Yes we d-i-i-i-d!' I wailed and sat up howling my eyes out, feeling betrayed as well as upset.

Mum came over and sat on the bed and held me. 'There, there,' she said, 'He wanted to know if you were all right. Are you?'

'Yes,' I said,' 'I just banged my knee.' I showed it to her, 'Ow! Ow - Oooh!' Now it hurt when I moved and was turning the most vivid bluish purple, 'and some of my toggles were torn off my jacket '

'Never mind about the jacket, but you need something cold on that knee for a while, don't you think?'

I nodded. Of course, Mum knew about first aid. She went downstairs, and after a few minutes brought back some ice wrapped in a towel and a glass of water, an Anadin and a cup of hot sweet tea. She wrapped the towel with the ice in it round my knee. 'No more than fifteen minutes with this,' she said, 'it's mainly to stop the swelling.'

'And so the bed doesn't get wet,' I joked. Being Mum, she giggled. Now I come to think of it, she always was a giggler.

'That's more like you,' she said, ' I've spoken to Len,' (Martin's dad)' and told him you'll survive. Now take that Anadin with the water, it should help you to sleep and get over the shock.'

'Thank you Mum, I'll ring Martin tomorrow.'

At that moment I did not feel like speaking to anyone, except my lovely Mum. I wondered if Dad knew and if he was angry with me and Martin. Or just me...or just Martin... or just angry.

The next day I spoke to Martin and he said he had to tell his parents because his leg hurt so much and his dad had noticed some damage to the bike. He had a huge graze on his thigh and his mum who had been a nurse, insisted he let her help him wash it clean. 'It really stung,' he said, 'I yelled my head off and it still hurts now.'

The duffel coat was repaired and my knee slowly healed, but it has always given me the odd twinge and I call it my 'motorbike knee.'

186.

I am not sure when I next rode on the bike but Martin's dad suggested we did not leave it too long in case one or both of us lost our nerve.

The summer holidays ended and it was time to make some serious decisions about the future. I applied to the speech and drama colleges with teaching courses in London and waited for their replies.

29

Meanwhile

Apart from seeing my boyfriend and doing art project work for my A Levels and reading, there was so much more going on in my teenage years, much of it to do with music.

Music was now an even larger part of my life. There was a record shop in town with little booths, where you could squeeze in with a friend and listen to the records you were thinking of buying. I now had a record player on which I could load several EP's at once from my growing collection

I took it for granted, but looking back, I now realise it was a good time for my generation. Records became cheaper and it was so easy to acquire our own copies of the hits we heard on the radio.

From early childhood I'd loved popular songs. If you want to see a list of my favourites see: **Pop Songs** at the back of the book.

***

As far as I was concerned, '*208 - your station of the stars*' Radio Luxembourg, was still my favourite station to listen to late at night. The signal was still not strong, so the sound could fade which was a problem under the bedclothes, but I managed to keep up with the Top Twenty.

I continued to enjoy the BBC radio programmes that I mentioned earlier, but now I was keen to listen to as much drama as possible. I remember some of the plays which I loved. The Third programme broadcast classic plays by Chekhov and Ibsen and John Wyndham's stories were dramatised. *The Kraken Wakes* terrified me as well as *The day of the Triffids*.

There was one play that affected me greatly. I just cannot remember the full title, but I know it contained a man's name, followed by, *Fallout Shelter*. This play reflected our deep fear of nuclear war and the government advice given to us on how to survive an attack. There were pamphlets on how to build a fallout shelter especially designed to protect the occupants from radioactive debris resulting from a nuclear explosion.

The radio play was about a man who built a fallout shelter that had enough room for others. He offered places to neighbours and acquaintances, but they all laughed at his fear and refused. Suddenly there was a threat of war and on going to take cover in his shelter, he finds it crowded with the people who had previously rejected him. They now told him there was no room. A cautionary tale for the nuclear age.

**

In the 1950's television broadcasting was very different to what we see today. For several years only BBC1 could be received and less than fourteen per cent of the population had television sets. It was the broadcast of the Coronation in 1953 that massively increased interest in television and the number of households with sets shot up. From the beginning, the hours people watched were tightly controlled by the Postmaster General.

On weekdays, television broadcasting was permitted between 9am and 11pm with no more than 2 hours before 1pm. There was also an hour of no broadcasting between 6pm and 7pm for the purpose of duping young children that the programmes were over and it was time for bed. It was known as the 'toddlers' truce.'

The rules were less stringent at weekends. A maximum of eight hours was allowed on Saturdays and seven and three-quarter-hours on Sundays. Also on Sundays, between 2pm and 4pm, programmes were intended for adults, as the expectation was that children would be at Sunday School.

So between the Postmaster General and my father, any television programmes I saw before the mid 1950's would not have been at home but at a friend's or a neighbour's house. When our father relented we only received the BBC channel. ITV, which began transmitting in 1955, was denied us for years. Martin's family had both and the television was on at his place most of the time.

(If you want to see the programmes I watched, see: **Television** at the back of the book.)

**

About this time I took to knitting and made some baby clothes for Peter which were quick and easy to finish. I then knitted larger items and made

189.

myself a black jumper, the first of many I would wear in my life and a long cardigan in a peachy-orange coloured jumbo wool with brass looking buttons. It was a mistake.

The cardigan was so heavy that after its first gentle wash it 'dropped' and ever after drooped around my knees. I hardly ever wore it. I also knitted Martin a red jumbo wool sweater but his kept its shape very well.

I was often busy with the sewing machine, mainly making dresses. The material for one was bright red and it was designed with a rather clever swathed bit over one shoulder, for which I needed Mum's help.

Another one was a 50's classic style with a boat shaped neck and almost circular skirt. The cotton material was turquoise with white stars. I also made a more complicated creation, which was in a pale pink with a drawn daisy design on it. It was fitting to just above the knee with a deep flounce all the way round. In my Bardot phase I also made myself a red check gingham skirt with shoulder straps. When a photographer came to take a family group photograph, he asked me if I would mind taking the straps down because they were so vivid. Honestly! It was going to be a black and white photograph.

Throughout all those years I had a camera, although I only used it sporadically. I now regret I did not have the sense to make a visual record of my art projects, but I took enough photographs to create a patchy record of those years.

30

Upper 6
September 1958 – September 1959

Well, this is it: my last year at school, now I have to pass my A Levels in French, English and Art, in order to secure a place at a London college next September. I hope that being young for my year will not scupper my chances of being accepted. Meanwhile, I must keep up to date with everything going on in theatre-land, pass my Grade 5 Speech and Drama examination and have time to see my boyfriend.

It is all doable.
I'm sure I can do it.
I just need to keep calm and not faint.

I was now a school prefect and my friend, Ann, who was very good at tennis and with whom I visited the greetings card company, was made Head Girl.

We were now entitled to use the prefects' room, where we could go to in breaks, or free periods, to make our own tea or coffee, read, play records, or just talk. It was at the top of one of the smaller school houses and could be cosy, especially in the winter term. For me it was a haven of peace, even more than the school library.

In the December of 1958 I passed my Grade 5 Speech & Drama exam and regretfully decided it was time to give up lessons with my speech tutor, of whom I had become very fond. From now on I had to concentrate on the mound of school work I had to get through if I were to pass my A Levels.

In English there were several set books, four of which were Shakespeare plays. Others included, Chaucer's *Squire's tale*, from which I learned to appreciate Middle English. Also, Spenser's *Faerie Queene* and Milton's *Samson Agonistes*. I first felt very negative about the latter, but later, enjoyed it. In addition we studied the Romantic poets: Keats, Shelley, Byron and Wordsworth and Jane Austen's *Mansfield Park* was on the curriculum (yawn) and Hazlitt's *Selected Essays* which I was slowly drawn to enjoy.

In Art, I was able to submit a piece of course work which would contribute to my final mark. I chose to design and build a set for a play and costumes for two main characters. The costumes had to be displayed on two miniature figures.

This was a gift to me, I had been enchanted by the magical designs for productions I'd seen at the Theatre Royal. My experience of seeing theatrical designs, such as Voytek's at the Nottingham Playhouse, gave me a broad view of what was achievable in set design.

I was also familiar with Leon Bakst's stage and costume designs for Diaghilev's *Ballets Russes* and although I knew I could never emulate them, they would be the inspiration for the characters I had in mind: Petruchio and Katharina from Shakespeare's The Taming of the Shrew.

What is more, I could make full use of my home grown carpentry and sewing skills!

As for French, well, it was all a bit hit and miss. I loved the literature: Corneille's *Le Cid,* Molière's *Tartuffe* and a more modern book, *Premier de Cordèe* by Roger Frison-Roche. However, I knew my grammar was inaccurate and sloppy, so I banked on getting a high mark in the literature.

It was about this time I received a letter that made my heart beat a lot faster. It was from the Central School of Speech & Drama, asking me to go for an interview and bring something to recite aloud.

The college was in Swiss Cottage in London. The enormity of the interview drove all other thoughts from my head. I have no recollection of how I got there, or what happened at the interview.

My hazy memory is that once I arrived I managed not to behave like a startled jelly. In fact, quite the reverse. The people conducting my interview were extremely pleasant and made me feel at ease. I went home and bit my nails for a week or two, until I received another letter to say that I had been accepted.

192.

I was overwhelmed with delight. I rang my lovely Speech and Drama teacher to thank her for her help and she wished me good luck. I still had to pass my A Levels, but I decided not to apply to any other colleges. As far as I was concerned that was IT!   I would pass my exams and I would go to Central.

Although a change was coming, life at home went on very much the same. I still played by my father's rules, but I was aware I would be out of his jurisdiction the next autumn. He was still sleeping downstairs. Mum was involved with little Peter, Dad went flying at weekends, Michael was continually playing with his electric train and I am not quite sure what Robert was doing in those days; but neither is he!

He certainly used to ride his bike, because I remember how furious he became if he had to pull it out from under all the other ones leaning on it in the garage. The air would turn blue. He did have a temper, but then, looking back, he had a lot of competition.

In between all the swotting and seeing my boyfriend, I stopped going to the Guides and the swimming club and concentrated on finishing my art project.

There were some essential administration tasks to deal with concerning going to college. Most important was securing grants from Nottingham County Council, one for the course tuition, plus a maintenance grant of some kind.

The former went smoothly but the latter was more of a problem as my maintenance grant amounted to £12 a week which was barely enough to pay for a room let alone travel and food. I looked round at other places but the hostels near the college were more than I could afford. I ended up making a provisional booking in an LCC women's hostel that was just off Sloane Square.

I would be sharing a room, but the hostel provided breakfast and supper and left me enough for tube fairs. My mother encouraged me to ask Dad if he could help me out. His discouraging reply was, 'I'm trying to get rid of my commitments, now.'

I blenched at the time and thought to myself, 'Well, what else did I expect?' I told Mum and she just said, 'Oh dear.' I did not wait to hear any more from her and went up to my room. I would just have to work my socks off to earn some money in the summer.

One positive aspect of all of this was that Martin had been offered a place at Imperial College London on the Mechanical Engineering degree course, so once we were both in London we might be able to pool our funds. As it so happened he received a more substantial maintenance grant than I did.

I soldiered on, revising and building my model set for *The Taming of the Shrew*. Initially I built most of it at home, but it was proving very difficult to carry it to and from school, as it was so cumbersome. I could only take it on the bus if I occupied two front seats upstairs. So, finally I left it at school and worked on it there.

The figures were less of a problem. They were about ten inches high and were each fixed on a wooden stand using wire as an armature. I created the bodies of the figures by using layers of papier maché; all that puppet making came in useful and it worked well. They looked even better when the clothes and hair were added. Petruchio's over the knees leather boots were a triumph!

I was still reading magazines like *Plays and Players* and keeping my ears and eyes open for any news about the theatre and films. A play, *Waiting for Godot*, by an Irish writer, Samuel Beckett, had created a storm of controversy. A brilliant young director, Peter Hall, had risked his reputation by agreeing to take on the job and had been highly criticised by most critics when audiences had walked out. Nobody seemed to understand it and it was described as meaningless and absurd, but it was challenging the safe and traditional.

Also, the harsh reality of ordinary people's lives was being reflected in new plays and books. A local Nottingham writer, Alan Sillitoe, wrote a best-selling novel, *Saturday Night and Sunday Morning*, about a self-centred youth who worked in the Raleigh bicycle factory. Albert Finney starred as the central character when the book was made into a highly successful film.

John Osborne's play, *Look Back in Anger*, was regarded as the first to break the bubble of conventional and romantic plays. I had read the publicity and thought that it was all rather exciting.

There were other terms, like 'Kitchen Sink Drama' and 'Angry Young men,' that were floating around as well as new playwrights' names: Arnold Wesker, (*The Kitchen, Chicken Soup with Barley.*), Shelagh Delany (*A Taste of Honey*) and Harold Pinter (*The Birthday Party*). There were also books such as *Room At The Top* by John Braine and *Billy Liar* by Keith Waterhouse. My cultural world was fizzing and exploding and I loved it.

The A Level Exams were in the last two weeks of June and the first in July. I had worked hard for them and felt I had done my best. I was free!

And so were all my friends. There were parties and noisy evenings and for the first time rather a lot of alcohol consumed. I was not old enough to buy drinks in a pub, but many of my friends were. Martin and I got drunk on gin one evening, in a red telephone box. I could pack a lot in before being home by 10.30pm!

Quite a lot of us smoked; there were no warnings about the true toxicity of cigarettes and for a while I used a cigarette holder which I thought was very stylish.

Although the exams were over I was not entirely free from school. Some of us were involved in putting on a production for the drama competition. We had agreed to present *A Phoenix too Frequent* by Christopher Fry as the staging was simple and there were only three in the cast.

It is set in a tomb at night where Dyamene, the grieving widow and her maid Doto are waiting to be entombed with Dynamene's dead husband. Tegeus-Chromis, the sentry, is on guard outside.

I was the producer and I designed programmes for the judges. The cast were excellent, as well as the backstage and design team. We had such a good time rehearsing.

It is a wonderfully humorous play and just the sort of thing to be involved in after all the stress of the previous weeks. We did not win but the judges' comments in the School magazine were brilliant:

'.....*U.VI.A's performance of A Phoenix too Frequent was beautifully staged and acted and the School much enjoyed its sparkling wit'*.....

195.

It was a terrific note on which to end my schooldays, obliterating the final moment when I lined up with the other girls to shake hands and say goodbye to Miss Milford, and she said to me, 'Goodbye Ann' and I had to quietly remind her of my actual name. I had been there nine years.

So...

That was it. All I had to do now was cross my fingers and hope I had passed my exams. My friends were in the same situation, including Martin. Oddly, I recall nothing of that summer, whether I worked (most probably) went on holiday (possibly) or just hung around at home (highly unlikely) is a mystery. I was in some kind of suspended animation, where all experience was irrelevant, while I waited for the curtain to go up on the next act.

But I do remember my relationship with my parents was not too good; I am not sure they approved of my liaison with Martin and Dad was as strict as ever. Well, they probably had good reason to worry what Martin and I got up to, but Carol and Roger were in exactly the same situation and Roger was always welcome at Carol's home. Much as I loved everyone at home I just had to get away.

I passed all my exams and so did Martin. The colleges were informed of our success, also Nottingham County Council, so the grants would be forthcoming. I confirmed my room at the L.C.C. Women's Hostel in Cadogan Square - just round the corner from Sloane Square.

About this time I was increasingly aware that my world was changing for ever. It was 1959 and my schooldays were coming to an end. Most people left school at fifteen and there were jobs for everyone. Millions of young people now had money to spend. No wonder the sales of records, clothes, make-up, cigarettes and cinema-going boomed.

Personally, I was still going to be hard up for the next few years. Only about four percent of young people went on to further education and I couldn't wait to be one of them.

In September I packed a huge suitcase of clothes, books and all the things I might need in my new life in London. The night before I left, my dear mum had given me an envelope containing £25 to 'help me out'.

Martin's dad had offered me a lift and the next morning, after

196.

saying goodbye to my family, he and Martin dropped me off at the station. Martin and I were going to meet up again in London as he was riding the motorbike down there. Having the bike in London would save him the cost of tube fairs from Wimbledon, where he was staying, to Imperial College in Kensington.

So there I stood, in the booking hall in Nottingham Midland Station. London beckoned and I was going to be part of it!

Postscript

Actually, that last part is a pack of lies. Martin wanted us to go together to London on the motorbike, but we had been expressly forbidden to do so by ALL our parents.

So, he went back home with his dad, saddled up his motorbike with his worldly goods in the panniers, apart from the ones I had in my huge suitcase and returned to the Midland station.

After removing my overnight stuff and crash helmet, I put my suitcase on the train to London. I think the system was called Red Star and it was much cheaper than the train fare.

We would be able to collect the case the next day at St. Pancras as we had allowed an extra day to do so. I did not have to wait for long until Martin appeared on the forecourt on the bike.

We drove all the way to London and we were fine - as was the weather. There was far less traffic than there is today and we were sensible enough to have a couple of breaks. Finally we manoeuvred our way through London to Chelsea and Cadogan Square.

Martin saw me into the reception area at the hostel and then he went on to Wimbledon. The hostel was warm and welcoming after the chilly journey. I was sharing a room with one other woman. I could barely believe I was there, but after ringing home from the hostel phone and telling them all was well, I had some supper and slept like a log.

Martin came to the hostel the next day, without the bike, and we went to St Pancras to collect the suitcase. After leaving it in my room we set off to explore the local area, Sloane Street, Sloane Square with the Royal Court Theatre and the King's Road, where I saw Mary Quant's shop, Bazaar.

The buses were red and there were some rather grand cars. The pavements were thronged with people hurrying by, or stopping to window shop. My mind buzzed with excitement and relief and a sudden sense of freedom. There was so much to see and explore.

The next day I was going to catch the tube to the Central School of Speech and Drama in Swiss Cottage. Home seemed a million miles away and I was in my very own personal heaven.

APPENDIX
The A-Z of my Town
Nottingham

This A to Z list is how it exists in my memory.

A - is for:

Albert Hall, the splendid Edwardian building where we held our school annual Prize giving evenings and sang songs to our parents. The elderly chairman of the governors, Dr Swinnerton, often made a speech and everyone laughed politely when he made a joke. Also, I remember going to a fascinating Faraday lecture there. The speaker explained how telephone systems worked by using tubes and bright coloured ping pong balls

A is also for the **Arboretum**, the park behind my school, where in my late schooldays I walked through on my way home. There, I was inspired to paint a picture in oils, now lost, of an urn overflowing with summer flowers.

A disturbing incident once happened to me there. When I was in one of the first forms I won a prize and two of the senior girls were assigned to escort me to Sisson and Parker's, the big book shop in Nottingham, to choose my prize. I chose a book on British birds. When we were on our way back I saw a naked man in the bushes. I said to my two escorts, 'Did you see that man? He had no clothes on.' and they asked where. I said 'Behind the bushes, back there.' We hurried back to the school gate and they went to tell one of the senior teachers. I was so innocent, it meant nothing to me, but I have not forgotten it.

B - is for:
Burton's Arcade, immediately behind the town hall. It always looked lovely at Christmas time with all the festive lights shining. Burton's was a

grand food emporium, with a luxurious line in groceries such as exotic sounding cheeses and smoked hams. Mum sometimes bought Melton Mowbray Pork Pies there, which were the best I have ever tasted.

B is also for **Boots**, the biggest chemist shop in town, which was appropriate, as Jesse Boot, a local philanthropist, had built up the business of selling herbal remedies he had inherited, into a nationwide chain of shops.

C - is for:

Castle - Nottingham Castle, high up on **Castle Rock** which housed a not very interesting museum of local memorabilia.

C for the Caves in the Castle Rock which tunnelled as far as the shops in the Derby Road.

C is also for the coffee bars that opened when I was a teenager. One was called El Toreador. The coffee machines were very noisy and made new types of coffee such as Cappuccinos and Espressos.

C is also for County football team whose club colours were black and white. The team was known as the Magpies.

Also for **Cinemas** such as:

The Odeon, a large one on Angel Row, with big swishy curtains. I saw *Gone With the Wind* there with Mum and *South Pacific* in Todd A-O, which was shown on a very wide screen with superior sound. It also had a restaurant, where, when I was young, we sometimes went to have Saturday lunch. I liked their mushy peas.

Also the Scala cinema on Market Street which often showed X rated films. I saw an awful film there called *Camp on Blood Island*.

Then there was the Mechanics Institute cinema, which was opposite the Victoria station. I saw Walt Disney's *Peter Pan* there and I was a bit snooty about it beforehand, because I did not believe you could make a cartoon of such a lovely story. Afterwards I had to admit I really enjoyed it.

Not forgetting the Tudor cinema in West Bridgford which I visited many times, including when I was a teenager, to see a late re-run of Disney's *Snow White*. The film gave me ghastly nightmares about the witch shrieking from the top of the crag.

C also for the depressing Nottingham **Canal**, which we occasionally caught glimpses of from the top of the bus as we neared the Midland station.

D - is for:

Dixon and Parker, the school outfitters, sometimes know as 'D and P's' where Mum and I went to buy my school uniform.

E - is for:

The **Empire Palace**, an old fashioned variety theatre, which was adjacent to the much grander Theatre Royal. I was in a Girl Guides show there; all I had to do was walk on in a line, turn and face the audience and salute and walk off again. I remember the footlights were very bright.

E also for **Edwalton**, the village where I went to the evening service and had confirmation classes with the Reverend E.Sheeran and joined the 1st Edwalton Girl Guide Company.

Not forgetting E for **Ellesmere Road** where our house was built on the corner with Haileybury Road.

F – is for:

The Forest, the great open space of playing fields where Goose Fair was held every autumn. Hooray!

F also for Nottingham **Forest** football team, red and white colours, and for Football Fans in their hundreds who walked along Arkwright Street and over Trent Bridge holding up the traffic.

G - is for:

Griffin and Spalding where Mum and I sometimes went to look for sewing patterns and where I worked as a waitress and supervisor.

And for **Goose** fair which arrived for only a few days each autumn and was fantastic.

H - is for:

Haileybury Road, that ran alongside our house. When we first looked at the site of our house-to-be, Haileybury Road was not much more than a track with big grey stones showing here and there above the dark coloured gravel. There is a photo of me riding my new bike on it and one of those grey stones must have been the one I badly banged my head on when playing cricket with the boys.

I - is for:

The **Ice Rink** where I went a few times to learn to skate and never became much good at it, but Torvill and Dean did.

J - is for:

Jessops where Mum helped me choose my first bra and also where she bought me a royal blue swagger coat which was in fashion at the time - and I loved it.

J is also for the Jesse Gray school which we saw being built on the field across the road.

K - is for:

The Kardomah, a posh cafe along from Griffin and Spalding which I only went to once.

L - is for:

Lenton Boulevard which, despite its pretentious name, I remember as being a very long boring road which did not seem to go anywhere.

Also the **Lace** factory I visited when there were very few of them left. I remember asking for some Nottingham lace in a prestigious haberdashers in Nottingham. It was for my brother's Belgian pen friend to take home with him. 'Oh no duck,' said the assistant, 'You can't get Nottingham Lace in Nottingham.'

M - is for:

The **Mac Fisheries** shop near the 24 bus stop on the Old Market Square.

And for the **Mansfield Road** where I caught the trolley bus into town on my way home from school.

M is also for the **Mikado** which was another smart cafe near Griffin & Spalding and which people called 'the Mik.'

And for the **Meadows** which was a scruffier part of Nottingham and for **Musters Road**, which was just across the school playing field. It was a long straight road which went all the way down the hill, through West Bridgford and almost all the way to Trent Bridge.

N - is for:

Nottingham - Hooray!

And the **National** Westminster Bank, where I often waited with a parent while they queued up to withdraw money. It was also where I had my first 'real' money savings box. It was shaped like a small book, about the same size as a Filofax. The long edge opposite the spine was shiny metal in which were there was a coin sized slot with teeth. If I changed my mind when a coin was half through the slot, the teeth grabbed it and I could not pull it back. There was also a little round hole to poke rolled up notes through. To open it I had to go into the bank. The idea was that the contents would be deposited in a savings account but I always kept some back for spending.

O - is for:

The **Old Market Square**, where the trolley buses and motor buses turned around. It was a place to sit on the public benches, to relax and to meet people - it was also the original site of the Goose fair. The Town Hall was on the East side of the square. Castle Rock was a few streets away to the West and the three theatres were a short walk up from the North side.

Gangs of Teddy boys or 'Teds' gathered in the square in the evenings and if Mum and I had been to the theatre she was very wary of them and always said she'd felt safer in London at night than she did in Nottingham.

I had not thought about it at the time, but the Old Market Square really was the hub of the City.

P - is for:

The **Playhouse** - a small repertory theatre which I loved. I saw some wonderful shows there, and sometimes I went with Mum and her theatre group. Plays I particularly remember are *Blizzard, The Winter's Tale, The Teahouse of the August Moon, Ten little Indians,* and a very funny pantomime of *Jack and the Beanstalk* with new lyrics set to Gilbert and Sullivan's music.

John Harrison and Val May directed many of the productions I saw and there was a group of young actors who to me, became the Playhouse 'family', Daphne Slater, Ruth Myers, Dennis Quilley, Graham Crowden, Peter Duguid, Patricia Healey and Vivien Merchant among others. The set designer Voytek became famous. When I was in the 6th form I was offered a part time job there but it was too much on top of A Level work.

P is also for the Palais de Danse where for a while I went to Saturday morning ballroom dance classes and heard a 'Dragnet' recording for the first time.

P is also for: **Players** cigarette factory - where some of the High School boys used to work in the holidays. They said the cheapest cigarettes, were made from the sweepings on the floor.

Not forgetting the **Portland Baths** where I went to the swimming club on Friday evenings

Q - is for:

Queues for the bus when I needed to get home on time at night.

R - is for:

Robin Hood, our legendary local hero. There is a statue of him, complete with longbow, near the castle but he looked a bit too podgy for my liking.

R is also for The **Raleigh** Bicycle factory I once visited and was mesmerised by the stunning changing colours the handle bars went through in the process of finally being covered in shiny chrome. The company was named after the street where the bicycles were first made.

And for **Redmayne and Todd** the large sports shop

R is also for the **Railway** bridge on Boundary Road beneath which the steam trains puffed on their way from London to Nottingham and places further North. For a while we collected their numbers and filled in our I-Spy books. At night you could see the coal fire glowing in the driver's cab and the carriages were all lit up. This did not last forever though; the railway line was closed and the cutting is now part of a nature walk.

S - is for:

Stations, Victoria **Station** which is now a shopping centre and the Midland **Station** where I used to arrive when returning from London.

And for **Sisson & Parker** the book and stationery shop where I bought pens, paints, paintbrushes, paper and other items I needed for art lessons.

T - is for:

The **Town Hall**, a grand looking building with pillars and a dome and wide steps leading up to the main entrance. A stone lion sat on either side of these wide steps. One year when it was the Nottingham University Student's Rag week, someone rang up the police to say the students were painting the lions red. The students always dressed up and did silly things during Rag Week and they also raised a lot of money for charity. This turned out to be a student jape; certainly some students were painting the lions red, but on paper.

Also **T** is for the **Theatre Royal** where mum took me to the ballet and we went to pantomimes and when I was older I went on my own to matinées and sat in the Gods - in heaven! I saw many productions including one with Richard Attenborough and Sheila Sim in the cast of rather silly who-dunnit. Mum was very impressed that I had seen them.

And for the **Theatrical** shop which sold all manner of moustaches and disguises and tricks and clucking chicken imitators. Costumes could be hired there too. It was where I bought Leichner stage make up and big tubs of 'Crowes Cremine' the theatrical make up remover.

Also **T** is for the **River Trent** which flooded quite frequently.

And for **Trent** Bridge which I travelled over many times.

Also for the **T.B.I.** (**Trent** Bridge Inn) which overlooked the **Trent** Bridge Cricket ground where **Test** matches were played. When we were in the 6th form, two of my friends from school had a night out with two of the Pakistan team.

And for **Tobys**, a shop on Friar Lane, which sold lovely things to give people as special presents.

U - is for

The **University** where one summer my friend Kay and I went rowing on the lake. Kay caught a crab in a spectacular fashion and we could not stop laughing.

V - is for:

Valley Road - where the terminus was for the number 11 bus which I used catch until the number 24 came up the hill.

Also for the **Victoria Embankmen**t on the River Trent. It had wide shallow concrete steps down to the water along from Trent Bridge. Between the steps and the road at the top there was a grassy verge. It was a lovely part of the river, but I did not go there very often although I could see it from the top of the bus on my way to school.

W - is for:

Woolworths which I loved. It was a huge shop and had thin creaky wooden floorboards and everything was cheap. It was the first shop I saw with a 'Pik and Mix' sweet counter.

X - is for:

the kisses on the backs of love letters to boys we fancied.

Y - is for:

Ye Olde Trip to Jerusalem Inn, a pub which was built under the castle Rock with stone walls. One corner I remember had a low curved stone roof over a table. A small wooden ball hung from the centre of the low roof and was used to knock over table skittles.

There was one story that this was the Inn where the Crusaders called on their way to the Holy land. However, the most common story was that it was where Christian pilgrims stopped on their way to Jerusalem. 'Trip' then meant 'Stop'.

Ye Olde Salutation Inn was another very old establishment, and was built on top of a network of caves as was **The Bell Inn** where the cellars are all carved out of sandstone.

Z - is for:

Z is for **Zebra** crossings which were introduced in Nottingham when I was nine years old.

Radio Comedy
The programmes I remember

ITMA (It's that man again) Starred Tommy Handley. It ran from 1939-49.

Much Binding in the Marsh, set in a mythical RAF station, 1944-54.

Take it from Here, with Jimmy Edwards, June Whitfield and Dick Bentley 1948-60. Years later, when I worked at the BBC, June Whitfield and I would occasionally get each others' mail.

Ray's a Laugh, with Kitty Bluett and Ted Ray 1949-61.

Al Read, was a one man show in the 1950's & 60's. I loved this series. Al Read played many different characters, one of them a loud rough householder, who in one sketch, with a nod to the arrival of television, opened the door to one of Al's meeker character and bellowed (in a Northern accent) *'Coom in, sit down, shut up, it's on.'*

Life of Bliss, with George Cole and his dog Psyche 1953.

Variety Playhouse, Compèred by Vic Oliver 1953- 63.

Hancock's half hour, starring the immortal Tony Hancock 1954-56.

Life with the Lyons, a sit-com starring the Lyons family 1951-61.

Pop Songs
Pop Songs I remember

Buttons & Bows, (Bob Hope) *Ghost Riders in the Sky*, (Frankie Laine).
Baby it's cold Outside, (Margaret Whiting & Johnny Mercer).
Music, Music, Music, Teresa Brewer *Mona Lisa*, (Nat King Cole).
Mule train, Riders in the sky, Cool Water, Granada, A woman in Love,
High Noon, I believe, Rawhide, (Frankie Laine).
Singing in the Rain, Little White Cloud that Cried, Walking my Baby back
Home, (Johnny Ray).
I love Paris, (Doris Day).
Diamonds are a Girl's Best Friend, (Marilyn Monroe).
How Much is that Doggie in the Window? (Lita Rosa).
Swedish Rhapsody (Percy Faith).I still have the single!
Rock around the Clock, Shake Rattle & Roll, See you Later Alligator,
Everybody Razzle Dazzle, (Bill Haley).
Sh – Boom, (The Chords) I love this!
Fly me to the Moon, (Kaye Ballard).
Secret Love, (Doris Day).
Let him Go, Let him Tarry, (Ruby Murray).
Cherry Pink & Apple Blossom White, (Eddie Calvert).
Only You, The Great Pretender, Twilight Time (The Platters) I still have the
single!
Unchained Melody, The man from Laramie, (Jimmy Young).
The Finger of Suspicion, Christmas Alphabet, Mr Sandman,
A Blossom Fell, Wonder who's Kissing her Now (Dickie Valentine) I thought
he was wonderful.
Maybelline, Roll over Beethoven, Rock & Roll Music, Johnny be Good,
(Chuck Berry).
Give me the Moonlight, Green Door, The Garden of Eden (Frankie
Vaughan).

Why do fools fall in Love (Frankie Lymon and the Teenagers).

Rock with the Cavemen, Elevator Rock, Singing the Blues, Nairobi, Only man on the Island, I puts the Lightie on, Little White Bull
(Tommy Steele).

Hound Dog, Don't be cruel, Heart break Hotel, Blue Suede Shoes Let me be your Teddy Bear, Loving you, Jailhouse Rock,
(Elvis Presley).

Love letters in the Sand (Pat Boone).

That'll be the day, Peggy Sue, Rave On, Not Fade away, Oh Boy, It Doesn't matter any More, Maybe Baby, Baby I don't Care, Well All Right
(Buddy Holly).

Tutti Frutti, Long tall Sally, Slippin & Slidin, Rip it up, Good Golly Miss Molly, Lucille, The girl can't help it (Little Richard).

Bye bye Love, Wake up little Susie, Devoted to You, All I have to do is Dream, Til I kissed You, Take a message to Mary, Cathy's clown
(The Everly Brothers).

Who's sorry now? Stupid Cupid, Lipstick on you collar (Connie Francis).

Move it, Living Doll, Travelling light (Cliff Richard).

What do you want to Make those Eyes at me For? (Emile Ford & the Checkmates).

Only have eyes for you (Flamingos).

Summer Place (Percy Faith).

What do you want, if you don't want money? (Adam Faith).

Television
The programmes I remember

All programmes were in black and white until Wimbledon 1967.

Watch with Mother was an umbrella title from 1953-65. I saw many of these programmes when my young brothers watched them after lunch in the holidays. They included a variety of characters: *Andy Pandy*, was a marionette doll who was joined by a *Teddy bear* and a *Rag Doll* called *Looby Loo*. Interestingly, these programmes were first shown live in 1950 and then twenty six episodes of 15 minutes duration were filmed, in black and white and constantly repeated thereafter.

Muffin the Mule, 1946-55 was a marionette donkey which performed on top of a piano played by Annette Mills. She interpreted Muffin's wishes for the young viewers.

The Flowerpot Men, 1952-60 were marionette puppets of two little men, *Bill and Ben*, constructed from flower pots and *Little Weed*, a small smiling sunflower. They spoke in their own language of 'Oddle Poddle' and one of their catch phrases was 'Flobbalob.' Each programme signed off with the narrator saying, 'I think the little house knew something about it! Don't you?'

Ivor the Engine, 1958-63 was stop frame animation, lovely programmes produced by Smallfilms for the BBC

Crackerjack, 1955-84, This was a great entertainment show for school age children. Once it moved to Fridays, it always began with, 'It's Friday, it's five o'clock. . . It's Crackerjack!' There was an excited studio audience and when anyone in the cast said, 'Crackerjack' they all yelled, 'CRACKERJACK' at the top of their lungs. There were games and sketches and music, and for a while a quiz, called 'Double or Drop.' Each of three contestants was given a toy prize to hold for each question answered correctly. If they were incorrect they were given a cabbage. They were out of the game if they dropped any of the items awarded or received a third cabbage. The winner won a bag of toys and the other two contestants received Crackerjack propelling pencils, which were highly prized. I loved watching it, even when I was much older

Blue Peter, 1958 to present day. I was never really a big fan of Blue Peter, but I was aware of their huge charity collections and always tried to collect for friends who wanted to contribute.

The Six-Five Special, began in February 1957. It was a rock and roll show, at 5 past 6pm on a Saturday evening on BBC TV. It was planned to only make six programmes, but proved so popular the series became open ended. I watched it whenever I could.

Juke Box Jury, 1959-67, was on Saturday nights. It was a panel show of personalities who listened to new pop recordings and judged them to be either a 'hit' or a 'miss'. David Jacobs was chairman. I did not often get the chance to see this as I was usually out on Saturday nights. At one point it had 12 million viewers.

Hancock's half hour, 1954-61 on radio and TV was, hilarious and unforgettable

Drake's Progress, 1957-58, starred Charlie Drake, with his catchphrase, 'Hello my darlings'

Come Dancing, 1949-83, was yesterday's 'Strictly come Dancing'. Peter West, was the first presenter and the frocks were magnificent, *'every sequin sewn on by hand'*,

This is your life, 1955-2007 was originally presented by Eamon Andrews.

The Good Old Days, 1953-83. I often watched this with Mum; she loved it.

Grandstand, 1958-2007, was on Saturday afternoons. The first presenter was Peter Dimmock. I can still remember the brilliant signature tune.

Panorama, 1953, presented by Richard Dimbleby from 1954, was hard hitting, sometimes controversial, investigative journalism from around the world. In 1959 Robin Day took over and although I did not have the opportunity to watch it often, I do remember the fuss about the hoax Panorama broadcast on April 1st 1957. It was a documentary of the spaghetti harvest in Switzerland. The switchboard was jammed with viewers who had been April Fooled!

The Sky at Night, was presented by the indefatigable Patrick Moore from

1957 – 2013. I was fascinated by the night sky and watched this whenever I could.

Whicker's World, was presented by Alan Whicker from 1958-68 on BBCTV then 1968-92 on ITV. This characterful presenter made some outstanding documentary programmes.

Zoo Quest from 1954-63 was the first nature programme to feature David Attenborough. I watched this when I could.

Dixon of Dock Green was from 1955-76 with Jack Warner as Dixon. He introduced each episode by directly addressing the viewers with his famous: 'Good Evening all' and signed out at the end with 'Good night all'. I remember enjoying these, they were a relaxing watch

The Adventures of Robin Hood, 1955-60. Richard Greene starred and 143 episodes were filmed and shown on ITV. The signature tune and opening titles are carved into my memory.

Little Women, 1950 The BBC broadcast six episodes, all live productions, (none recorded). Also, in 1958, six new episodes were made, of which all recordings exist. This is the version I remember, especially Andrée Melly who played Jo.

Jo's Boys In 1959 the BBC broadcast seven episodes, of which I saw few, as I had begun drama college.

Jane Eyre, in 1956, the BBC broadcast six episodes, starring Stanley Baker who played Rochester, and Daphne Slater played Jane. This was the year Daphne Slater joined the original Nottingham Playhouse.

Pride and Prejudice, 1958, BBC. I remember Alan Badel as Mr Darcy.

Saturday Playhouse, ran from 1958-61. These were hour long live dramas, only one still exists.

Sunday Night Theatre, 1950-59. These were one off live dramas, up to two hours long on Sunday evenings and repeated on Thursdays – live.

This was the decade of the *Quatermass* plays, none of which I saw, I have no idea why. Of course home recording machines weren't available to the public for decades.

In September 1959 I left home for college and watched very little television at all for three years.

214.

ACKNOWLEDGEMENTS

First my deep thanks to my son Steven who had the idea and inspired me to write this tale of my young life, for him and Oliver and Cassie.

Many thanks to my dear brothers, Michael for his alternative and humorous view of our childhood together; Robert for his unfailing and detailed research on all things flying and family and Peter for his tremendous support when I was flagging. Thanks also to my cousin Mercedes who helped me fill in gaps in my knowledge about the war years and the family tree.

Thanks to my school friends: Carol Chell, particularly for her memories of school drama activities and Anne Crawford (née Yates) now living in Vancouver and her recollections of school life.

And on the subject of school days, I am grateful for the swift response from Mrs Katie Haddow at the Nottingham Girls' High School to my query about school drama competitions in the 50's.

My thanks also fly overseas to South Auckland, to Sheila Whelan (née Knight) for all things local to my home life; anything to to do with Guides (including photographs), and for being such a great companion on our Lakes holiday.

Thanks to my dear friend Sue Boland who helped me prepare the book for publication.

Finally, my thanks and love to Mike Molloy, for his patient support, advice and expertise in all things literary.

EPILOGUE

SUNNY SLOANE SQUARE
Written February 1973

Sunny Sloane Square
Where I caught my first tube train
To college
And sat with businessmen
Charladies
Students
and girls
In sunlight that strobed
Through the gaps
In the tunnel
Each morning.

Sunny Sloane Square
Where we started that long night
On the tiles
And walked through Kensington
Piccadilly
Mayfair
and Soho
In streetlight and rain
And we dozed
On the first train
Next morning

Sunny Sloane Square
Where we just caught a glimpse of
That Kennedy
And cheered with the rest of them

216.

Americans
Tourists
and he
In dusklight looked godlike
Then shot down
One morning

Sunny Sloane Square
Where I drive through occasionally
Just passing
With children on holiday
Or T.V.
Producers
on visits
To show them the places
in London

Reminds me
Of Kennedy, Mary Quant, night time
and King's Road and Royal Court
and leaves in the square
Sloane Square

Where I caught my first tube train
to college
One morning

Chapter 1

Dad in uniform 1941

Big Granny in the garden

H/MS Stevens 1927

Dad and Judy at 7 months

Mum and Dad's Wedding June 7th 1940

Dad and Judy in 1945

Judy in 1944

Little Granny and Grandad on pier

Judy in 1945

Mum and Judy at 7 months

Chapter 2

My family in 1946

Judy's
first school photo

Judy & Michael with cousins
Mercedes & Sarah

Judy's siren suit

Judy favourite bucket

Chapter 3

and I went on the
swings and Michael
went on the little roundabout
he put his bathing costume

September 9th Friday
I had a swim in the
morning and we went to
Mrs Plunketts in the afternoon
and we had tea there and
afterwards auntie Plunkett fed
her chickens and we went
to a farm.

September 10th Saturday
I went to Aldershot
in the morning and saw
Granny and Grandad and when
we came back at night
time we saw all the lights

September 11th Sunday
My cousins came to-day
and there mother and father
came they came just be....

Seaside holiday diary

My fairy cycle 1948

Cover of Sunny Stories
magazine

Chapter 4

Left to right
Food ration book for tea, children's
clothes and Camp coffee label.

Left: Judy, Dad
and Michael

Right and below:
Judy and Michael

Chapter 5

Wasteland, where our
house was to be built, 1949

5.1.50.

Dear Mummy and Daddy
I Like it very much
at the Nursing home.
I am quite good friends
with Dorothy now.
Thank you very much
for the nice card
you sent me.
Yours

sincerely

Judith

x x x x y x x

Letter to parents
when in nursing home after
tonsillectomy

Our new house 'Upavon'

Chapter 6

David Shearn and Judy.

Katherine, Judy and Alison.

Judy and a new bike.

Michael, David, Judy, Sheila, Alison,
Jane Wells & Paddy the dog.

Lines in 1950

Peter Benham and Judy in Lancing in 1950

Chapter 7 & 9

Robert and Michael
on Lancing beach

Family photograph in 1951

D&P advertisement

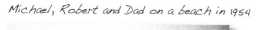

Michael, Robert and Dad on a beach in 1954

Judy, Mercedes, friend, Michael
and Stewart

Granny knitting on the beach.

Dad and one of his
amazing sandcastles

Chapter 12, 16, 17, 18, 19

Christmas 1955

Judy in 1955 with
short hair!

Guide Camp badge,
heather patrol.

Lower 4M in 1954

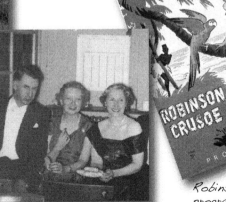

Guide Camp.

February 1952,
evening do.
My father on the
far left, mother,
third from left

Robinson Crusoe
programme.

Chapter 20, 21, 23

Auster plane, Judy Summer 1954

Well dressing 1955.

Derby airways

The Silver Curlew. Judy as a yokel,
second from right

My drawing of
'a view from a
window' with no
texture!

Chapter 24, 25, 27

Christmas 1955 'The Lady's not for burning'. Judy far left

Skiffle group at Burnside Hall

Kay, Welly, Yates winter 1956

Judy Arboretum 1957

Owl school Christmas card

School building Christmas card

Chapter 28, 29

Judy posing in a pink dress.

Lake trip with Sheila.

Judy's design for drama competition programme cover

Mum's Civil Defence Certicate 1958.

Us kids 1958.

Garage view from my bedroom

Mother's professional career

WYN STEVENS

Mum's picture
in a programme

Mum in an advertisement

Mum is 2nd from
the left

Mum is on
2nd row,
5th from right

Cover photographs:

Front cover:
Judy two and half years 1944
Sheila and Judy, Lakes holiday 1958

Back cover:
Top left to right:
Sister and brother Wyn and Bert, my mother and uncle.
Grandad Taylor as young Hussar
Middle left to right:
From play programme 1959
Big Granny (Stevens)
Bottom left to right:
H C M Stevens (grandad)
Little Granny and Grandad Taylor

Printed in Great Britain
by Amazon